Books are to be returned on or before
the last date bel

KT-511-247

Musicals
in Focus

by
Paul Terry

Rhinegold Publishing Ltd
241 Shaftesbury Avenue
London WC2H 8TF

052212

113566

THE HENLEY COLLEGE LIBRARY

Also available from Rhinegold Publishing:
Madonna: *The Immaculate Collection* in Focus
The Who: *Who's Next* in Focus
Danny Elfman: *Batman* in Focus
John Barry: *Goldfinger* in Focus
Baroque Music in Focus
Film Music in Focus
Modernism in Focus
Romanticism in Focus

Rhinegold Music Study Guides
(series editor: Paul Terry)
Students' Guides to GCSE, AS and A2 Music for the AQA, Edexcel and OCR Specifications
Listening Tests for GCSE, AS and A2 Music for the AQA, Edexcel and OCR Specifications
A Student's Guide to GCSE Music for the WJEC Specification

Key Stage 3 Elements
Key Stage 3 Listening Tests: Books 1 and 2
Music Literacy Workbook
Music Composition Workbook
A Student's Guide to Harmony and Counterpoint

Rhinegold Education also publishes Classroom Music, Teaching Drama, Rhinegold Dictionary of Music in
Sound, Rhinegold Guide to Music Education, and study guides for Classical Civilisation, Drama and
Theatre Studies, Performance Studies, and Religious Studies.

First published 2008 in Great Britain by Rhinegold Publishing Ltd
241 Shaftesbury Avenue
London WC2H 8TF
Telephone: 020 7333 1720
Fax: 020 7333 1765
www.rhinegold.co.uk

© Rhinegold Publishing Ltd 2008

All rights reserved. No part of this publication may be reproduced, stored in a retrieval system, or
transmitted in any form or by any means, electronic, mechanical, photocopying, recording or otherwise,
without the prior permission of Rhinegold Publishing Ltd.

Rhinegold Publishing Ltd has used its best efforts in preparing this guide. It does not assume, and hereby
disclaims, any liability to any party for loss or damage caused by errors or omissions in the guide whether
such errors or omissions result from negligence, accident or other cause.

Paul Terry: Musicals in Focus
British Library Cataloguing in Publication Data.
A catalogue record for this book is available from the British Library.

ISBN: 978-1-906178-24-6

Printed in Great Britain by Thanet Press Ltd

Contents

The author

Paul Terry's love of musicals first developed when, as a teenager, he was appointed musical director for a series of shows at his local amateur theatre in south-east London. As a music teacher he conducted productions of *Oliver!*, *Cabaret*, *Joseph and the Amazing Technicolor Dreamcoat* and *Oh, What a Lovely War*. As well as training children for professional productions of musicals, Terry has worked with adults on amateur productions of *Oklahoma!*, *Kiss Me, Kate*, *Kismet* and *Paint Your Wagon*. Paul is series editor of Rhinegold's music study guides and, as a former chief examiner in music for two A-level boards, he has co-authored many books on A-level and GCSE music

Acknowledgements

Paul Terry would like to thank Professor Linda L. Sturtz for reading an early draft of the text and would like to dedicate this book to the memory of H. Marshall Palmer, who inspired a love of music and the stage in so many of his pupils.

The author would also like to thank John Pymm for his advice and suggestions as well as Elisabeth Boulton, Lucien Jenkins, Ben Robbins, Sabine Wolf and Chris Elcombe of Rhinegold Publishing for their assistance throughout the editing and production process.

Copyright acknowledgements

The author and publishers are grateful to the following publishers for permission to use printed excerpts from their publications:

'Give my regards to Broadway': Words and music by George M. Cohan. © 1941 Edward B Marks Music Co. B Feldman & Co Ltd, London W8 5SW. Reproduced by permission of International Music Publications Ltd (a trading name of Faber Music Ltd). All rights reserved.

'Tea for two' and 'I want to be happy': Words by Irving Caesar, music by Vincent Youmans. © 1924 Harms Inc. Warner/Chappell Music Ltd, London W6 8BS. Reproduced by permission of Faber Music Ltd. All rights reserved.

'Can't help lovin' dat man': Words by Oscar Hammerstein, music by Jerome Kern. © 1927 T B Harms Company (50%). Warner/Chappell Music Ltd, London W6 8BS. Reproduced by permission of Faber Music Ltd. All rights reserved.

'Captain Andy' ('Coloured chorus'): Words by Oscar Hammerstein, music by Jerome Kern. © 1927 T B Harms Company and Polygram International Music Publishing (50%). Warner/Chappell Music Ltd, London W6 8BS. Reproduced by permission of Faber Music Ltd. All rights reserved.

'Cotton blossom' and 'Ol' man river': Words by Oscar Hammerstein, music by Jerome Kern. © 1927 T B Harms Company and Universal Music Publishing (50%). Warner/Chappell Music Ltd, London W6 8BS. Reproduced by permission of Faber Music Ltd. All rights reserved.

'Let's do it (let's fall in love)': Words and music by Cole Porter. © 1928 (renewed) WB Music Corp. All rights administered by Warner/Chappell Music Ltd. London W6 8BS. Reproduced by permission.

''S wonderful': Words and music by George and Ira Gershwin. © 1927 (renewed) WB Music Corp. All rights administered by Warner/Chappell Music Ltd. London W6 8BS. Reproduced by permission.

'Embraceable you': Words and music by George and Ira Gershwin. © 1930 (renewed) WB Music Corp. All rights administered by Warner/Chappell Music Ltd. London W6 8BS. Reproduced by permission.

'Anything goes': Music and words by Cole Porter. © 1934 Warner Bros Inc. Warner/Chappell North America Ltd, London W6 8BS. Reproduced by permission of Faber Music Ltd. All rights reserved.

'Too darn hot': Music and words by Cole Porter. © 1949 Chappell & Co Inc. Warner/Chappell North America Ltd, London W6 8BS. Reproduced by permission of Faber Music Ltd. All rights reserved

'Recitative', 'Porgy' and 'It ain't necessarily so': Words and music by George Gershwin, Ira Gershwin, DuBose Heyward and Dorothy Heyward. © 1935 Gershwin Publishing Corporation. Warner/Chappell North America, London W6 8BS. Reproduced by permission of Faber Music Ltd. All rights reserved.

'Oh, what a beautiful mornin'': Lyrics by Oscar Hammerstein II. Music by Richard Rodgers. Copyright © 1943 by WILLIAMSON MUSIC. This arrangement Copyright © 2008 by WILLIAMSON MUSIC. Copyright renewed.

'Anything you can do': Words and music by Irving Berlin. © 1946 Irving Berlin Music Corp. Warner/Chappell Music Ltd, London W6 8BS. Reproduced by permission of Faber Music Ltd. All rights reserved.

'Wouldn't it be loverly': Words by Alan Jay Lerner, music by Frederick Loewe. © 1956 Chappell & Co Inc. Warner/Chappell North America Ltd, London W6 8BS. Reproduced by permission of Faber Music Ltd. All rights reserved.

'Prologue (motifs)', 'Mambo (motifs)', 'Cha Cha (motifs)', 'Maria', 'America', 'Cool'. 'I have a love' and 'Somewhere': Music by Leonard Bernstein, words by Stephen Sondheim. © Copyright 1956, 1957, 1959 by the Estate of Leonard Bernstein and Stephen Sondheim. Copyright renewed. Leonard Bernstein Music Publishing Company LLC, Publishers. Boosey & Hawkes, Sole agent. International copyright secured.

'Willkommen': Music by John Kander, words by Fred Ebb. © 1966 Trio Music Company Incorporated, USA/Alley Music Corporation, USA. Carlin Music Corporation. Used by permission of Music Sales Limited. All rights reserved. International copyright secured.

'Aquarius': Words by James Rado and Gerome Ragni, music by Galt MacDermot. © 1960 Channel-H-Prod Inc and United Artists Music Co Inc. EMI United Partnership Ltd (publishing) and Alfred Publishing Co (print). Administered in Europe by Faber Music Ltd. All rights reserved.

'Prepare ye the way of the lord': Music and words by Stephen Schwartz. © 1972 Herald Square Music Company/New Cadenza Music Corporation, USA. Carlin Music Corporation. Used by permission of Music Sales Limited. All rights reserved. International copyright secured.

'Overture': Music by Andrew Lloyd Webber, words by Tim Rice. © Copyright Leeds Music Limited. Universal/MCA Music Limited. Used by permission of Music Sales Limited. All rights reserved. International copyright secured.

'What's the buzz', 'Everything's alright', 'The temple' and 'Gethsemane': Music by Andrew Lloyd Webber, words by Tim Rice. © Copyright MCA Music Limited. Universal/MCA Music Limited. Used by permission of Music Sales Limited. All rights reserved. International copyright secured.

'No place like London' and 'Johanna': Words and music by Stephen Sondheim. © 1979 Rilting Music Inc. Warner/Chappell North America Ltd, London W6 8BS. Reproduced by permission of Faber Music Ltd. All rights reserved.

'I dreamed a dream' and 'On my own': Music by Claude-Michel Schönberg, original lyrics by Alain Boublil and Jean-Marc Natel, English lyrics by Herbert Kretzmer. © Copyright (music and lyrics) 1980 Editions Musicales Alain Boublil. English lyrics © Copyright 1985 Alain Boublil Music Limited (ASCAP). Used by permission of Music Sales Limited. All rights reserved. International copyright secured.

'Can you feel the love tonight': Words by Tim Rice, music by Elton John. © 2002 Wonderland Music Company Inc. Warner/Chappell Artemis Music Ltd, London W6 8BS. Reproduced by permission of Faber Music Ltd. All rights reserved.

'The lion sleeps tonight': Written by Luigi Creatore, Hugo Peretti, George D. Weiss and Solomon Linda. ©1961. Renewed 1989 and assigned to Abilene Music c/o Memory Lane Music Ltd. All rights reserved. International copyright secured. Printed with permission.

Preface

This evening, at the end of a typical day in March 2008, there are professional productions of 25 different musicals being staged in the West End of London, in theatres ranging in size from just a few hundred seats to more than 2,000. And in America, 29 different musicals are running tonight in the Broadway area of New York. Yet more musicals, known as 'off Broadway' and 'off West End' productions, can be heard in other parts of both these cities.

London and New York have long been famous centres of excellence for musicals, providing employment for a large number of actors, singers, dancers, orchestras and supporting staff. As well as offering high-standard entertainment for both locals and visitors, musicals play an important role in the economy, with many tourists coming to stay in these great cosmopolitan cities with the intention of going to several shows during their visit.

Professional productions of musicals are staged in, or tour to, many other towns and cities around the world, and every year there are countless amateur productions in local theatres, schools and colleges.

This book traces the development of the musical, exploring why it has become such a popular form of theatrical entertainment. It looks at changes in style during the 80-year history of the genre and shows why a series of significant works have become so influential. It begins by investigating how musicals are constructed and what features are commonly found in most shows.

Recordings and DVD films of most of the musicals mentioned in the book are readily available (some suggestions are given in the Chronology and Resources chapter at the end of the book) but remember that the best way to experience the thrills and excitement of a good musical is to go to the theatre to see a live production.

1
Setting the scene

A musical is a work for stage or screen in which singing plays an essential role in telling the story. The word 'musical' came into common use in the second half of the 20th century as a shortened form of terms such as 'musical play', 'musical comedy' and 'musical film' that had been used in earlier years.

Most musicals were originally written for live performance in a theatre, although many have later been adapted for the cinema, often involving much rewriting of the original stage version in the process. Some were conceived as **musical films** from the outset, such as *Mary Poppins* and *The Lion King* – both of these films were subsequently adapted as stage musicals.

There is often spoken dialogue between the songs in a musical, although some shows (such as *Les Misérables* and *The Phantom of the Opera*) are sung throughout. Such works are described as **through-composed** or **sung-through**.

In addition to solo singers, there may be a **chorus** of voices who sing together, and many productions make use of dancing and elaborate spectacle.

The accompaniment may be provided by anything from a piano or a small group of musicians to a large band or orchestra. In a theatre the players are usually positioned below the level of the stage, largely out of sight of the audience, in a sunken area known as 'the pit' – that is why they are called the **pit band** or **pit orchestra**.

Most of the features outlined above can also be found in opera. Indeed, musicals such as *Sweeney Todd* and *On the Town* have been staged in London's opera houses. Both operas and musicals can be through-composed or both may contain spoken dialogue; musicals need not necessarily be light-hearted (*Les Misérables* and *Sweeney Todd* are not) any more than operas are always tragic. However, there are some important differences between the two:

- Musicals, unlike opera, contain music composed in a broadly popular style
- Musicals generally use professional actors who can sing, while opera uses professional singers who can act
- Because few actors have the technique to project their singing voice above the sound of a band in a large theatre, voices are generally amplified in today's musicals, while they are generally not in opera.

Although musicals are composed in a popular style, this seldom reflects the chart music of the day – it is usually more 'middle of the road', drawing on a variety of well-tested ideas from the past and placing a lot of value on memorable tunes that the audience can hum as they leave the theatre. This is inevitable since musicals take years to plan, finance, write, rehearse and produce, and, once staged, a successful show may run for 20 years or more, making it impossible to reflect the latest rock and dance fashions. Also, many musicals are set in past times (such as the Victorian London of *Oliver!*) in which the very latest rock styles might seem out of place.

This stylistic time lag works to the advantage of the musical, as the familiar sound of well-established, tuneful styles can help the show appeal to a wide audience, and is one of the main reasons for the extraordinary popularity of musicals.

Some technical terms

The starting point for a musical is the **book** (sometimes called the **libretto**, which is Italian for 'little book'). It lists the characters, identifies the settings, and contains both the spoken and sung text, thus outlining the dramatic structure of the show. It also either includes the **lyrics** (the words for the songs) or points out where these are to be added by another writer. It is unusual, although not unknown, for composers of musicals to write their own words.

Most musicals are adapted from existing literary works – often novels (as in the case of *Oliver!* and *The Phantom of the Opera*) or stage plays (*Oklahoma!* and *My Fair Lady*). The sources for some well-known musicals are given in the Chronology and Resources chapter on page 81.

A good book is essential for success; situations that allow characters to experience a wide range of emotions tend to generate the best and most varied songs, but these need to arise naturally from the plot, and transitions from spoken dialogue to singing need to be as smooth as possible. Approaching a song with words such as '…but that's how I feel. Let me tell you about it…' can leave a modern audience cringing.

The writer of the book also has to plan a suitable structure (see below) in which the drama is effectively paced. Adapting the book from a novel means material has to be selected carefully to fit the available performance time. Music can enhance the emotional content, but it can also slow the action down, requiring many cuts to be made from the original novel or play. The author of the book needs considerable skill in identifying the real essence of the drama to condense this into a relatively small number of pages.

The **score** contains all of the music for the show. Some composers produce a **full score**, containing the notes to be played by every instrument and from which parts for the individual musicians can be copied. Others write a melody and an outline accompaniment, leaving it to assistants to write an orchestration and sometimes to add additional music. There have been a few composers (notably Irving Berlin and Lionel Bart) who could read little or no music, and who thus depended heavily on others to produce a working score.

Full scores of musicals are not generally available on sale, in order to prevent unlicensed performances; most can only be obtained on hire as part of a licensing agreement with the rights holder. Older musicals are often available as a **vocal score**, showing all the voice parts, but reducing the accompaniment onto two staves suitable for a pianist to play during rehearsals. Unfortunately, a number of more recent musicals are available only as a selection of highlights (in vocal score) that fail to show the structure of the entire show. Details of the scores (and DVD films) available for a number of famous musicals are shown in the Chronology and Resources chapter on page 81, but it is important to remember that musicals are often revised for different productions (and are almost always rewritten if filmed), so it can be almost impossible to arrive at a definitive text in which what you see exactly matches what you hear.

Other key figures involved in creating a musical include an **impresario** (a person who often initiates the original idea, commissions writers, plans finance, books the theatre and engages a production team), a director (in overall charge of the production), a set designer, costume designer and lighting designer, and a **choreographer** who is responsible for planning and staging the dance routines.

The first public performance of a musical is called its **premiere** or opening night, before which there may be a **preview** for the press and invited guests. Sometimes there may be a complete preview run in a provincial theatre, giving the opportunity for changes to be made before the show moves to Broadway or the West End. Once under way, the musical will be staged almost daily, and may well tour other cities after the Broadway or West End run is over. Popular musicals often receive a **revival** some years later, in which the original production may be changed quite dramatically.

Types of musical

The **musical comedy** was the earliest type of musical. In works such as *No, No, Nanette* (discussed on pages 27–29) a light-hearted story forms a showcase for an entertaining variety of songs and dances that can sometimes seem to interrupt the plot rather than carry it forward.

In a **book musical**, the work is devised so that the musical numbers seem to arise naturally out of the action. They serve to develop the characters and carry the story forward, as in *Oklahoma!*, discussed on pages 44–47.

A **concept musical** is based more on an idea than a story, with songs that tend to comment on the action rather than carrying it forward. For example, the most memorable feature of *Chicago* (1975) is its dazzling evocation of a jazz-age night-club, complete with on-stage big band and a succession of show-stopping songs, rather than the story that links these aspects together.

A **compilation musical** (or 'jukebox musical') consists of existing songs linked by a slender plot. The success of *Mamma Mia!* (a tribute to the songs of Abba) in 1999 has led to a number of such works, but a much earlier example is *Singin' in the Rain* (1952), a musical film written around a back-catalogue of songs from previous decades.

The structure of a musical

Most musicals are a little over two hours in length and many fall into a well-established pattern of two sections (**acts**) separated by an interval that gives the audience an opportunity to stretch their legs and the theatre management a chance to generate additional income from the sale of drinks, snacks and souvenirs.

The writer of the book and the composer usually jointly decide the position of the musical items (called **numbers**) in the show. The overture (if there is one) and the **opening number** set the mood and both are often left to be composed after the rest of the musical has been written. Some musicals begin with a **production number** – a big tune with lots of singers and dancers, vivid costumes, loud accompaniment and brilliant lighting. Cole Porter's *Kiss Me, Kate* (1948) is a typical example – the audience is immediately drawn into the production with a welcoming opening number, 'Another openin', another show… A chance for stage-folks to say Hello!'

Production numbers are also used to highlight key moments in the show. When the wealthy widow Dolly Levi returns to her favourite restaurant in Act 2 of *Hello, Dolly!* (1964), the head waiter doesn't greet her with a spoken 'Good evening, madam, it's nice to see you again'; instead she is welcomed by the entire restaurant staff singing 'Hello, Dolly, well hello, Dolly, it's so nice to have you back where you belong', the famous production number also providing the **title song** of the musical.

In a two-act musical, it is generally considered desirable for the first act to be the longer of the two, and to end by leaving the audience wanting more. Sometimes this effect is achieved by posing cliffhanger questions that will be resolved in the second act, and sometimes it provides another opportunity for a production number.

The conclusion (**finale**) of the second act is even more important. Dramatically, it needs to resolve, preferably in an unexpected way, any questions and conflicts that have arisen earlier. Musically, it is desirable to reach a climax and, to ensure the memorability of the main tunes in the work, composers often include a **reprise** (repeat, possibly in shortened form) of one or more of their best previous numbers. A typical example is the finale of *Oklahoma!*, which creates a sense of completion and complete circularity by using a full-company reprise of the show's opening song, 'Oh, what a beautiful morning'.

There are many other ways to handle a finale. Some musicals end with another production number, others conclude with a substantial section of continuous music called a **scena** (a scene) in which the final questions of the plot are unravelled, often underscored by highly dramatic music. The ending of *Oliver!* provides a good example – the villain (Bill Sykes) tries to escape by using the young Oliver Twist as a hostage but is shot in the attempt, after which the curtain falls on the image of the manipulative Fagin escaping to continue his life of crime. Being far from the sort of rousing ending usually expected in musicals, the curtain then rises again for a reprise of the jolliest tunes from the show. Few musicals end with the unremitting sense of tragedy that colours the conclusion of many famous operas – in most musicals, a key objective is to ensure the audience leave the theatre in a happy mood.

The author of the book also has to consider how songs should arise from the action, especially if they are preceded by spoken dialogue. There needs to be a stimulus for an actor to break into song – for instance, it could be that the character has reached an important decision or some new insight that demands reflection on events – and the song needs to move the story forward rather than just being an entertaining interruption. At the same time, the best songs from musicals are often designed to be hits in their own right, and therefore still need to make sense when they are taken out of the context of the stage show. Similarly, there needs to be a reason for introducing a chorus or dancers, such as setting the action in a bustling street market, or at a party or dance.

Numbers in a musical can either be vocal or purely instrumental. The main types of vocal number are:

- Solo songs (sometimes with a refrain sung by the chorus)
- Duets for two soloists, and vocal **ensembles** for three or more soloists (trios, quartets etc.); again, with or without the chorus
- Scenes, usually involving several characters and often including changes of mood
- Choruses (including production numbers).

Songs (and duets) can reflect a huge variety of moods – one of the things that makes musicals so attractive – but certain common types can often be spotted:

- **Ballads** are slow – often they are love songs ('As long as he needs me' from *Oliver!*) or a reflection on events that have taken place ('Close every door to me' from *Joseph and the Amazing Technicolor Dreamcoat*)
- **Comedy songs** require great emphasis on getting the lyrics across clearly (as in 'Gee, Officer Krupke' from *West Side Story*)
- **Dramatic songs** (such as the title song of *The Phantom of the Opera*)
- **Novelty numbers** (such as 'Surrey with the fringe on top' from *Oklahoma!*, with a rhythm designed to reflect the clip-clop of a horse's hooves)
- **Charm songs** intended to endear a character to the audience (such as 'Wouldn't it be loverly?' from *My Fair Lady*)

- **Aspirational songs** (often starting with 'I want…' as in 'I want to be happy' from *No, No, Nanette*, or starting with 'If…' as in 'If I were a rich man' from *Fiddler on the Roof*)
- **Informational songs** (often starting with 'I am …' as in 'I am 16 going on 17' from *The Sound of Music*)
- **Inspirational songs** (such as 'Climb every mountain' from *The Sound of Music*).

Some other common vocal categories will be encountered later in this book (such as patter songs on page 18 and waltz-songs on pages 19–21).

Purely instrumental numbers in a musical may include any of the following:

- An **overture**: following the tradition of operetta many musicals open with a potpourri ('mixture') overture. These often start with a loud 'call to attention' to settle the audience, and then give a foretaste of the best tunes that will be heard later in the show, rather like a trailer in the cinema.
- **Incidental music**: often designed to cover scene changes. These days, theatres can usually, with the aid of technology, achieve a rapid and exciting scene-change (or transformation) in full view of the audience, and so such music may often be cut in modern productions. The term **entr'acte** is sometimes used for a number played between different acts or scenes.
- **Dances**: some musicals, such as *West Side Story*, have a strong dance element.
- **Play-out music**: a series of instrumental reprises played after the final curtain to reinforce the audience's memory of the best tunes as they leave the theatre.

Why are musicals so popular?

The sheer variety of possible answers to this simple question is indicative of why musicals have such wide appeal. Most musicals offer, in little more than two hours:

- A range of theatrical experiences, from moments of drama or even tragedy, through song and dance to vivid production numbers, often featuring stunning visual effects
- A variety of musical and emotional experiences, from the excitement of a live band or orchestra in the pit to human actors on stage, only yards away, delivering anything from intimate solo ballads to overwhelming full-company numbers
- Music in a broadly popular (middle of the road) style that appeals across the generations and attracts family audiences.

In addition, many of the most popular musicals offer a glimpse of societies beyond most people's everyday experiences, such as exotic locations (*Miss Saigon* or *South Pacific*), life in a bygone age (*Les Misérables* or *Cabaret*) or even pure fantasy (*Mary Poppins* or *Little Shop of Horrors*).

Musicals

But perhaps the most important reason for the popularity of musicals is the success of their invitation to audiences to 'dream the dream'. The lights go down, the curtain comes up and all sense of disbelief is suspended as eyes focus on the stage to watch the figure of the underdog overcome a series of obstacles and misfortunes to achieve a dream.

> I dreamed a dream in time gone by
> When hope was high
> And life worth living
> I dreamed that love would never die
> I dreamed that God would be forgiving ...
>
> *Les Misérables*

> I closed my eyes, drew back the curtain
> To see for certain, what I thought I knew.
> Far, far away, someone was weeping,
> But the world was sleeping.
> Any dream will do.
>
> *Joseph and the Amazing Technicolor Dreamcoat*

2
Origins of the musical

The modern musical developed in the 1920s, but its roots go back much further to two parallel traditions of theatrical entertainment in which music plays a central role:

- **Operetta** (or comic opera) in which musical numbers, mostly in a fairly light style, illustrate an amusing, topical or fanciful plot that runs throughout.
- **Variety shows** (including burlesque and vaudeville) in which songs are interspersed between dances, comic turns, magic acts and so forth, in a less structured fashion than operetta, with little in the way of a plot to link them.

Ballad opera

One of the earliest forerunners of the musical was *The Beggar's Opera* (1728), a satirical play based around popular songs of the day. The intention of its author, John Gay, was partly to poke fun at the fad for serious opera among London's upper-class theatre-goers. Such operas, written by Handel among others, were very formal, being sung in Italian throughout. In contrast, *The Beggar's Opera* is sung in English and uses spoken dialogue between the songs. Part of Gay's spoken prologue makes his intention clear: 'I have not made my Opera throughout unnatural, like those in vogue'.

The characters in the work are thieves and prostitutes, not the ancient rulers that were the usual subjects of Italian opera. Gay's work tackles issues of social inequality as well as lampooning Robert Walpole, Britain's first prime minister, taking a dig at financial corruption and suggesting that the moral values the play satirises are hypocritical. Audiences loved it, although these were much the same wealthy audiences that also attended the operas which were being ridiculed, for working people had neither the time nor the money to go to the theatre in the early 18th century.

Much of the music of *The Beggar's Opera* uses melodies, to which John Gay wrote new words, from the huge collection of popular and traditional tunes in *Wit and Mirth or Pills to Purge Melancholy*, the last volume of which had been published in 1720. Gay also freely filched tunes from various composers of the day, including Handel. The composer Johann Pepusch (like Handel, a German who had settled in London) wrote the overture and was also probably responsible for adding the simple bass parts that underpin the songs.

The songs used were known as ballads – stories in verse that could be sung to popular tunes. Long before being collected in *Wit and Mirth,* they had been sold as single sheets (called 'broadsheets') on the streets of London. Their subject matter was often topical and satirical, and the use of similar material in *The Beggar's Opera* has given rise to the term **ballad opera** for stage works of this sort.

Most of the songs in *The Beggar's Opera* are **strophic** – that is, the same tune is repeated for each verse. The following is the first half of a simple duet that consists of two verses to identical music, one for each singer – they don't sing together. It takes the form of a lively 'slanging match' between two of the leading female characters:

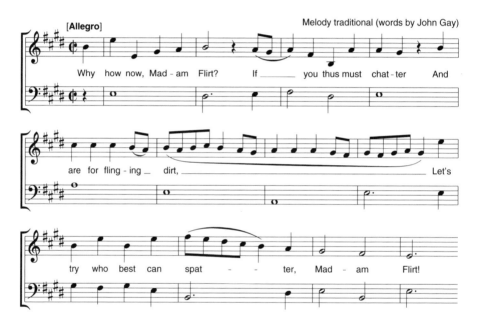

Although the words are Gay's, the tune is a popular song called *Gossip Joan* taken from *Wit and Mirth.* Most of the setting is **syllabic** (one note per syllable) but the long **melisma** (group of notes to the same syllable) on the word 'dirt' is an amusing parody of the type of florid operatic singing that Gay set out to caricature. *The Beggar's Opera* was enormously successful. Indeed, an enterprising publisher of the day even brought out a set of commemorative playing cards, each featuring a musical number from the show, rather like the souvenir T-shirts, mugs and albums that are often sold to help publicise successful musicals today.

The work was revived many times throughout the 18th century and was followed by a number of other ballad operas, although none were as successful as

The Beggar's Opera. Eventually Londoners' interest waned in favour of less satirical forms of theatrical musical entertainment, although the idea of stage works in which spoken dialogue alternates with sung numbers was pursued enthusiastically in Germany and Austria, where composers such as Mozart and Weber developed the *Singspiel* ('sung play') into a serious art form.

The Beggar's Opera was also a success in America, where it was first performed in New York in 1750, becoming the first-known professional musical production to be staged in that (then very small) city. Ballad opera remained popular in America for some years, finally being eclipsed by the minstrel shows (see page 22) of the early 19th century.

The Beggar's Opera has been restaged successfully in the 20th century – most notably including a run of 1,463 performances at the Lyric Theatre, Hammersmith, starting in 1920. Before then, however, the 19th century was to see the flowering of a new type of musical entertainment for the stage that was to have a more immediate impact on the development of the musical. The full text of *The Beggar's Opera*, without music, is available to study online at www.uoregon.edu/~rbear/beggar.html.

Operetta

Although the history of opera includes some brilliant comic masterpieces, such as Rossini's *Barber of Seville* (1816), by the middle of the 19th century a demand had developed for shorter but entertaining musical works for the stage. This demand was led by the growing middle-class audiences that could now afford to go to the theatre. They wanted some of the trappings of opera, including strong tunes and a colourful orchestral accompaniment, but sought amusing (if often implausible) plots, plenty of variety (preferably including some dancing), action that could be sped along by spoken dialogue between the musical numbers, and – above all – works written in the local language, rather than Italian, so that the jokes could be understood.

The result was operetta – a form of light opera that developed outside Italy, primarily in the cities of Paris, London and Vienna.

Paris

Although neither French by birth nor the inventor of operetta, Jacques Offenbach (1819–1880) was its first really successful composer, writing 100 such works to words by Ludovic Halévy and others. His first big success came in 1858 with *Orphée aux enfers* (Orpheus in the Underworld) in which the Greek myth is sent up – almost literally, for the gods ascend to Mount Olympus in a balloon at the end of the first act.

The entire work is essentially a middle-class jibe at the aristocratic taste for opera, the tragic Orpheus myth having been the subject of several serious operas. So, instead of being the singer of legend, Offenbach's Orpheus is a bad violinist, whose wife cannot stand his playing – he threatens her with a three-hour solo in their opening duet. One absurdity quickly leads to another as disguises cause mistaken identities and conspiracies go wrong. Along the way, the audience is entertained with storm effects, dances and transformation scenes. Being operetta, all ends happily – in place of the tragic conclusion of the original myth, the gods have a party and a wild dance:

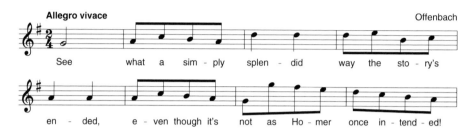

This is the saucy *can-can* (colloquial French for 'scandalous gossip'), a riotous popular dance style of the time, involving leg splits and high kicks that expose a good deal of the chorus girls' legs. This number from *Orpheus* is the most famous of all can-cans, but Offenbach seldom failed to include one in his later operettas. Other common features include waltz-songs (songs in waltz rhythm – see pages 19–21), potpourri overtures (often assembled by others) to whet the audience's appetite with a selection of melodies that will appear later, and reprises to ensure the memorability of the best tunes as well as to help give musical structure to the complete show.

After *Orpheus*, Offenbach consolidated his reputation with a string of successes that include:

- *La Belle Hélène* (1864) – another spoof on the ancient world
- *La Vie parisienne* (1866) – a much more modern story that opens in a railway station with the staff singing out the names of all the wonderful places in France that can be reached by train
- *La Grande-Duchesse de Gérolstein* (1867) – a political satire that centres on the havoc wreaked by the female ruler of a tiny and imaginery European state, who has a weakness for young men in uniform.

London

The success of *La Grande-Duchesse de Gérolstein* in London, where it was staged only seven months after its Paris premiere, generated a demand for native works of similar quality that would reflect a more English style of humour, and avoid some of the more risqué elements of French operetta.

This demand was satisfied by the impresario Richard D'Oyley Carte, who wanted a short work to share the bill with Offenbach's *La Périchole*. He commissioned the comedy writer W. S. Gilbert and the young composer Arthur Sullivan to create a one-act operetta. The result was *Trial by Jury* (1875) and its success launched Gilbert and Sullivan on a series of works known as the **Savoy operas**, named after the Savoy Theatre that Richard D'Oyley Carte later built for their production.

The pair were to write 12 more operettas together, the most famous of which include *H.M.S. Pinafore* (1878), *The Pirates of Penzance* (1879), *The Mikado* (1885), *The Yeomen of the Guard* (1888) and *The Gondoliers* (1889). These works proved to be enormously popular throughout the English-speaking world. They have stayed in the professional repertoire ever since, and form part of the core repertory of many amateur operatic groups.

The success of 'G&S', as this repertory is affectionately known, was in part due to Gilbert's particularly English sense of humour, which revelled in absurdity. The plot of *The Pirates of Penzance* revolves around a mis-hearing that resulted in Frederic, the male lead, being apprenticed until his 21st birthday as a pirate instead of a pilot. In a typically Gilbertian twist, he then discovers that he was born on 29 February in a leap year – so he will be in his eighties by the time he has had 21 birthdays.

Poking fun at officialdom is another essentially English trait found in the Savoy operas. *Pirates* includes a 'very model of a modern major-general', whose comprehensive grasp of matters intellectual is matched only by his total ignorance of things military, and a chorus of the most timid policemen imaginable. Similarly, *Pinafore* parodies desk-bound officials, with a First Lord of the Admirality who advises 'Stick close to your desks and never go sea, And you all may be rulers of the Queen's Navy!'. In *Iolanthe* (1882) the object of Gilbert's satire is no less than the entire House of Lords, who 'did nothing in particular, and did it very well'.

Gilbert had a love of puns, that can now sometimes seem dated, and implausible plots involving magic lozenges. However, he never fought shy of contemporary references. For example, the 1878 libretto of *Pinafore* makes clear reference to the newly-invented telephone, two years before it was even available in London:

> He'll hear no tone of the maiden he loves so well!
> No telephone communicates with his cell!

Other up-to-the-minute references have not stood the test of time so well. The audience at the first night of *Iolanthe* (1882) collapsed in laughter when they heard the heroine extol the virtues of the handsome and newly appointed head of the London fire brigade (who just happened to be in the audience):

> Oh, Captain Shaw, type of true love kept under,
> Could thy brigade with cold cascade quench my great love, I wonder?

Such dated references either have to be changed or explained in modern productions. However, Gilbert was capable of seizing on enduringly attractive rhymes ('in for a penny, in for a pound, it's love that makes the world go round') and phrases so memorable that they have entered the English language as sayings in their own right – for example, 'a short, sharp shock' and 'let the punishment fit the crime' (both from *The Mikado*), 'a policeman's lot is not a happy one' (*The Pirates of Penzance*) and 'What never? Well, hardly ever!' (*H.M.S. Pinafore*). Gilbert was also an accomplished theatrical director, and established very high standards in the production of the Savoy operas.

Equally important to the partnership was, of course, the music. Sullivan had great, but largely unfulfiled, ambitions to establish his reputation as a composer of serious music. However, his abilities to create sparkling melodies and write fluently in almost any style were just the sort of skills needed to give the interest and variety that made his operettas so popular. Thus, *Trial by Jury* includes a quartet ('A nice dilemma we have here') that effectively mimics the type of elaborate vocal ensemble popular in the operas of Donizetti, and a chorus of welcome from the sycophantic jury ('All hail great judge') that sounds almost as if it had leapt out of the pages of an oratorio by Handel. This gift for pastiche is evident in all of the Savoy operas. *The Mikado* contains a modern version of a madrigal ('Brightly dawns our wedding day'), *The Gondoliers* includes a vocal ensemble in the style of an ancient gavotte ('I am a courtier grave and serious'), and ends with castanets flying in a magnificent Spanish dance called a cachucha, while *The Sorcerer* (1877) includes an old-style minuet.

Most of Sullivan's operettas begin with a potpourri overture which, like Offenbach's, was often assembled at the last minute by an assistant. Also like Offenbach, many of his works include a waltz-song (see pages 19–21). All of the Savoy operas are noted for the variety of their vocal numbers, ranging from quasi-serious solo ballads and soliloquies to lively solos with choral refrains, duets, trios, elaborate ensembles and climactic finales. The chorus plays an important part in all of the works, and is one of the reasons why they have remained so popular with amateur groups.

A feature that was a particular speciality of G&S was the **patter song**. Usually written for the leading baritone, the object of these syllabic settings was to delight the audience by getting through a stream of tongue-twisting words as quickly as possible, as in the Major-General's song from *The Pirates of Penzance*:

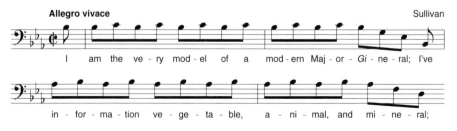

Numbers such as this were parodying the patter songs of Italian opera popular in the early 19th century, but they became associated with the Savoy operas to such an extent that Gilbert and Sullivan were able to parody themselves in *Ruddigore* (1887), in which a patter trio memorably ends with the lines:

> This particularly rapid, unintelligible patter
> Isn't generally heard, and if it is it doesn't matter!

Vienna

Austria's answer to Offenbach was Johann Strauss II, long known as the 'waltz king'. His third operetta, *Die Fledermaus* (The Bat) appeared in 1874. It was initially far from a triumph, perhaps because of its convoluted plot, but Strauss's music ensured that it would quickly become one of the best-loved operettas of the 19th century.

Die Fledermaus contains little of the pithy satire seen in many of the works discussed so far. It is essentially a domestic farce about a wealthy couple who spend much of the operetta deceiving each other about various indiscretions, only to find each other out by the end.

The centre-piece of the work is a grand masked ball – the traditional vehicle for a succession of mistaken identities and resulting mishaps – for which Strauss wrote a series of opulent dance-based songs, including a Hungarian *czardas* for the wife, who is out to trick her husband into flirting with her in the belief that she is a visiting countess from Hungary. At the ball the hapless husband catches the eye of an 'actress' (it is actually their own maid in disguise), and suggests to her that he feels sure they've met before. Her mocking response is 'Mein Herr Marquis' – popularly known as 'the laughing song' for obvious reasons. As can be seen from this short excerpt, Strauss did on occasion write demanding vocal lines of a type more associated with grand opera than operetta:

The masked ball also includes one of Strauss' most famous waltzes, shown in the second example on page 21. It should be clear by now that the **waltz-song** was an almost obligatory feature of operetta, and its popularity continued well into the age of the musical. The examples on page 21, by the three operetta composers discussed so far, illustrate some of the typical features of the waltz-song:

- They are in triple metre and move fairly briskly with a feel of one beat, not three, per bar
- The metre is emphasised by an 'oom-cha-cha' style of accompaniment in which the bass falls on the first beat and the accompanying chords on the remaining two beats of each bar
- They are based on units of 4 and 8 bars (such regularity being essential for the movements in formal dances such as the waltz, although waltz-songs are not necessarily accompanied by actual dancing)
- Their elegant melodies are often coloured by chromatic notes.

All three examples make prominent use of the sixth note of the major scale harmonised by tonic or dominant chords (marked *). This note belongs to neither chord but it adds colour to both and also serves to weaken the traditional key-defining role these chords had in classical music. The result is one of the most characteristic harmonic features of 19th- and early 20th-century popular music.

Johann Strauss II continued writing operettas until his death in 1899, achieving particular success with *Der Zigeunerbaron* (The Gypsy Baron) in 1885. The Viennese style of operetta continued into the 20th century with Franz Lehár. His best-known work is *Die lustige Witwe* ('The Merry Widow') of 1905, a tuneful and amusing account of a wealthy widow's attempts to find a new husband.

Lehár's operettas had a direct influence on the romantic musical comedies of the early 20th century. Indeed, if you listen to his dreamy hit song 'Dein ist mein ganzes Herz' (You are my heart's delight), you might well think it was from a musical rather than from his 1929 operetta *Das Land des Lächelns* (The Land of Smiles).

But the romantic legacy of operetta was only one of the strands that led to the musical. For the other, we must return to the 19th century to see what was happening in America.

Examples of the 19th-century waltz-song

American variety shows

The various types of variety show that became popular in America during the 19th century were also to influence the development of the musical. Emerging in the 1840s, the **minstrel show** consisted of comic acts, dances and songs performed by white (and later, after the abolition of slavery, also African-American) entertainers in 'blackface' – stage make-up used to give an unflattering caricature of a black face. The shows were mainly confined to the northern states, where they pandered to bigoted views of the South by portraying black Americans as ignorant, lazy stereotypes. But minstrelsy had one saving grace – it introduced a vibrant new style of popular music.

Many of the songs sung in minstrel shows are still remembered today, although their origins are sometimes unclear. Dan Emmett's Virginia Minstrels introduced the American public of the 1840s to *Polly Wolly Doodle* and *De Blue Tail Fly* – songs that are thought to have originated among slaves. Later Emmett introduced *Dixie*, which was almost certainly his own composition. Its bold marching style and simple but lively syncopations led to the adoption of *Dixie* as the unofficial anthem of the southern Confederacy in the American Civil War:

The most famous composer of minstrel songs was Stephen C. Foster (1826–1864), often described as 'the father of American music'. Following the success of his song *Oh Susanna* in 1847, Foster was commissioned to write for the Christy Minstrels, producing songs that range from the comic *Camptown Races* to the sentimental *Old Folks at Home* ('Way down upon the Swanee River').

Foster was keen that his 'plantation songs', as he called them, should avoid the more offensive aspects of minstrelsy and he instructed white singers not to mock slaves but to convey a sense of compassion for their plight. However, his lyrics were written in a thick mock African-American dialect, and there are occasional verses that really have to be removed from modern performances. Nevertheless, Foster's aim was realised in songs such as *Old Folks at Home*, which embodies a sense of universal longing that goes well beyond the confines of its original minstrel-show context.

Despite dying at the age of 37, Stephen C. Foster went on to write hits in a variety of other styles, including the waltz-song *Beautiful Dreamer*, the spiritual-like *Hard Times Come Again No More* and the Celtic-like *Jeannie with the Light*

Brown Hair. As minstrel shows started to fall from favour, Foster's legacy passed to James A. Bland, American popular music's first successful black composer, who wrote such minstrel hits as *Carry Me Back to Old Virginny* (1878) and *Oh, Dem Golden Slippers* (1879).

As minstrelsy declined, it was replaced in popularity by a new type of variety show that had emerged in the 1860s. The **burlesque** borrowed from the minstrel show's structure, with its combination of song, dance and comedy routines, but it had one important difference. Many of the performers were women – usually scantily-clad women. Variety remained the essence of these shows and, while there were usually some short sketches, there was often little sense of any overall storyline.

Burlesque quickly developed a reputation for risqué jokes, sexual innuendo, exotic acts such as woman contortionists, fire-eaters, and a chorus line of girls displaying as much flesh as could be got away with. Dances such as Offenbach's famous can-can were often an accompaniment to these so-called 'leg shows'.

Nevertheless, there are some burlesques (or 'extravaganzas') that can be seen as antecedents of the 20th-century musical. *The Black Crook* (1866) differs from most burlesques in that it has a connecting (if implausible and derivative) plot underpinned by some simple, often slightly saucy, songs gleaned from a variety of sources:

The main attractions of *The Black Crook* were visual, however – in particular, spectacular special effects and no less than 100 dancing girls in tights. As a consequence, the show ran for over a year at Broadway's largest theatre of the day (the 3,200-seat Niblo's Gardens), was revived eight times and toured for decades to come.

By the 1880s, the public in cities such as New York were seeking an alternative to tawdry minstrel shows and risqué burlesques – something more suitable for a family audience, although not necessarily as sophisticated as the Gilbert and Sullivan operettas that were by then all the rage in America.

The answer came with the advent of **vaudeville**. This was altogether more respectable than minstrelsy or burlesque as the range of unrelated acts on offer each evening might include pieces of light-classical music, lectures from celebrities and scenes from Shakespeare, as well as magical illusions, female impersonators, comedy acts, dancers, trained animals and popular songs.

Musicals

Popular music had started to become a commercial industry by about 1895. Increasing prosperity led to more families being able to afford a piano, and cheaper printing created a ready supply of sheet music to perform at home. Numerous songwriters and publishers established their base in a small area of New York that became known as **tin-pan alley**, possibly from the noise of dozens of pianists trying out the latest material. Vaudeville artists would team-up with publishers to plug their latest songs and by going to the theatre, audiences could, in the days before radio, be sure of hearing the latest hits.

One of the most successful vaudeville entertainers was George M. Cohan, whose first song was published in 1893 when he was only 15. Two years later his father put him in charge of the family act, which consisted of song-and-dance routines and comedy sketches. Following a dispute with one of the leading vaudeville impresarios of the day, Cohan decided to develop such material into complete musical comedies in their own right.

Musical comedy had become increasingly popular in the last quarter of the 19th century. Such shows reflected the humour and musical tastes of working-class people in everyday situations, and had very simple plots to link a vaudeville-like series of songs, dances and comedy routines. One of the first was *The Brook* (1879) in which five people go for a picnic and then produce from their hampers the costumes and props for their various performances. The songs in *The Brook* were all taken from other sources, but Cohan wrote his own material (songs and scripts) and achieved a much more unified result with his first big success *Little Johnny Jones* (1904), in which he also starred in the singing, tap-dancing lead role.

The story features an American jockey who comes to London. He is followed by his sweetheart (disguised as a man) who is keeping an eye on him. The jockey is falsely accused of fixing the result of the Epsom Derby – but all is resolved in the end and he marries his girl. The songs arise naturally from the action and include two hits that are still familiar today – 'I'm a Yankee-Doodle Dandy' and the syncopated march-song, 'Give my regards to Broadway', sung as Jones' liner leaves for New York without him:

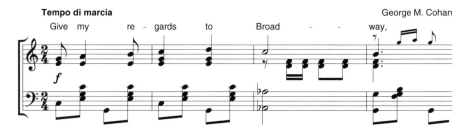

Little Johnny Jones is seldom performed today – even at the time reviewers felt it lacked the humour of some of Cohan's earlier musical comedies – but it is a work closer in form to a modern musical than any we have yet encountered.

The increasing success of tin-pan alley was bolstered in the first two decades of the 20th century by three factors:

- The arrival of exciting new styles of popular music such as ragtime
- The sale of gramophone records, which allowed recordings of songs to be heard in the home
- The appearance of a number of talented new songwriters, including Irving Berlin and Jerome Kern.

One of the outlets for the vast number of songs that was being produced was yet another new type of musical entertainment designed for the theatre – the **revue**. These plotless shows, the most famous of which were the long series of *Ziegfeld Follies*, drew on a number of elements from earlier types of music theatre, including chorus girls, songs and comedy sketches. By charging high seat prices, Florenz Ziegfeld was able to offer audiences a spectacular night's entertainment provided by the best performers and songwriters of the day – including Irving Berlin, Jerome Kern and Richard Rodgers, all of whom would go on to be key figures in the creation of the 20th-century musical. Ziegfeld himself went on to produce what many would regard as the first great musical – *Show Boat* (see page 30).

3

The pioneers

The First World War, which was so destructive in other ways, had surprisingly little impact on musical theatre in London. It was important to keep theatres open for the entertainment of troops home on leave, and to bolster the morale of the population in general. As a result, the musical comedy *Chu-Chin-Chow*, which opened halfway through the war in 1916, ran for 2,238 performances – the longest run in the history of London theatre before 1954. The war had even less effect on musical theatre in New York, which was far removed from the centre of conflict and where, in any case, America was only involved in the later stages of the war.

As a consequence, musical theatre emerged from the war in a good state to counter the considerable challenges it was to face in the 1920s, including the introduction of radio broadcasting, the rise of jazz and (by the end of the decade) the appearance of films with sound. Broadway was well equipped for forging a place for musical theatre among these advances in entertainment. There was a galaxy of talented composers and authors ready to respond to a variety of demand and, by the end of a decade of remarkable artistic development, a new form of theatrical entertainment – the **musical** – had made its mark.

Many of the works mentioned earlier in this book have some claim to being labelled as the first musical – later we shall investigate one that has a much stronger claim. Some theatrical historians would point to September 1925 as the birth of the musical. That month saw, within a space of seven days, the opening nights of:

- *Sunny*, with music by Jerome Kern and words by Oscar Hammerstein II
- *Dearest Enemy*, with music by Richard Rodgers and words by Lorenz Hart
- *The Vagabond King*, with music by Rudolf Friml
- *No, No, Nanette*, with music by Vincent Youmans.

The musicals of Jerome Kern, and of Rodgers and Hammerstein (who would eventually work together) will be considered later.

Rudolf Friml, born in Prague, perpetuated the tradition of Viennese operetta from the late 19th century. He moved to America and worked with such lyricists as Hammerstein and Otto Harbach (who also contributed to *Sunny* and *No, No, Nanette*), achieving considerable popular fame with numbers such as the 'Indian love call' from his 1924 operetta *Rose-Marie*. Friml eventually went on to write film music in the 1930s.

Several other composers continued in the same tradition. Sigmund Romberg was another immigrant from Europe who later turned to film music after achieving success with operettas such as *Lilac Time* (based on adaptations of Schubert's music) and more original works such as *The Student Prince* (1924) and *The Desert Song* (1926), the latter being turned into one of the first really successful musical films in 1929. Victor Herbert, who had studied music in Germany and played in the orchestra of Johann Strauss II in Vienna, is remembered for such works as *Babes in Toyland* (1903) – a musical counterpart to the 1900 *Wonderful Wizard of Oz* story by L. Frank Baum, that was to spawn countless adaptations over the years.

Vincent Youmans: *No, No, Nanette*

Despite receiving its official premiere in London, *No, No, Nanette* is an American musical with songs in a much more contemporary style than the nostalgic sound of Friml or Romberg. The experienced Otto Harbach helped playwright Frank Mandel produce the book (based on the latter's 1919 play, *My Lady Friends*); Irving Caesar (who had written the words for Gershwin's first hit song, *Swanee* in the same year) worked with Harbach on the lyrics, and the score was by Vincent Youmans – a tin-pan alley composer who had previously worked with the young Oscar Hammerstein II, who was to become one of the greatest lyricists of the 20th century.

The rather slight plot centres on Nanette, the young and wealthy heiress of a Bible publisher, who decides to run away from her overbearing parents to Atlantic City for a weekend of fun. There she discovers that her father has innocently given money to various beautiful women who are now trying to blackmail him, and that her mother is there attempting to find out what is going on. Needless to say, all the confusion is eventually dispelled – mother and father are reunited, and Nanette gets to marry her long-term boyfriend.

The most significant feature of *No, No, Nanette* is Youmans' music, rather than the script (in fact, modern productions use a rewritten version of the book made for a 1971 Broadway revival of the show). It includes two famous hit songs – 'Tea for two' (one of the most frequently-recorded tunes ever written) and 'I want to be happy'. Both reveal how popular music was developing a new style. Instead of long arching melodies (as seen in the waltz-songs on page 21), Youmans builds his songs around short, repeated musical figures that we might nowadays describe as 'riffs':

Similar short-breathed, repetitive phrases dominate the chorus of 'I want to be happy', shown in the example on the next page. The reason for this is simple – these are songs written for actors, rather than for specialist singers who can carry long-phrased melodies. In addition, the technique of building a song on the repetition and variation of a simple motif helps make the number all the more memorable to audiences. 'I want to be happy' also illustrates a musical form that was to dominate musicals, and most popular music, for decades to come – **32-bar song form**.

It is important to realise that 32-bar song form refers only to the structure of the chorus, not the entire song. However, the chorus is always the most memorable part and, outside of the show itself, the verses are often omitted – a practice that started because of the very limited recording time available on records in the 1920s. The 32-bar structure of the chorus falls into four eight-bar phrases:

A   The main melody
A   The main melody repeated to new words
B   A contrasting melody (known as the 'bridge' or 'release')
A   Another repeat of the main melody.

In musicals, these 32 bars are often sung twice – first by the soloist and then by the chorus – before the song continues with a second verse and chorus. Each verse has different lyrics, but the choruses normally all have the same words.

The attraction of 32-bar song form becomes clear when viewed from the audience's perspective – they hear something new (A), something familiar (A again), something new (B) and finally something which is by now very familiar (A for a third time).

Musically, the A sections are normally closed – meaning that they end with a perfect cadence in the tonic key, while the B section is open – meaning that it ends with an imperfect cadence to prepare the way for the final A phrase. In addition, the bridge is the most likely place for a brief modulation to a related key, and its lyrics often present a new slant on the main literary idea of the A section. All of these points are illustrated in the 'I want to be happy' excerpt on page 29.

Composers showed great ingenuity in varying this simple plan – for instance, the last phrase of 'Tea for two' starts on a climactic top note and continues with a different melodic contour to the first phrase, although it has the same insistent dotted rhythm – only coming back to the original idea in its last four bars. We could describe this as AABA[1] form. Occasionally the final phrase repeats the bridge (ABAB) or is totally different (AABC). More rarely, the initial repeat of the first phrase may be omitted, resulting in an ABA form. Some songs have an extended final phrase (often ten bars in length) to produce a more conclusive ending (another type of AABA[1] form).

Introduction

Moderately

Vincent Youmans

Verse

p | I am just an or - di - na - ry man, try - ing to work out life's hap - py plan;

The verse continues for 16 bars in all ... doing unto others as I'd like to have them doing unto me.
When I find a very lonely soul, to be kind becomes my only goal;
I feel so much better when I tell them my philosophy.

Chorus (in 32-bar song form)

A *p-f*

I want to be hap - py, but I won't be hap - py

'til I make you hap - py too. _____

A

Life's real - ly worth liv - ing when we are mirth giv - ing,

Why can't I give some to you? _____

B

When skies are grey and you say you are blue,

I'll send the sun smil - ing through. _____

A

I want to be hap - py, but I won't be hap - py

'til I make you hap - py too. _____

The entire song is then repeated with different words for the verse but the same words for the chorus.

The first half of the 20th century saw a wonderful flowering of popular song writing in the United States. Five composers, all near-contemporaries, stand out in the field of the musical:

Jerome Kern	(1885–1945)
Irving Berlin	(1888–1989)
Cole Porter	(1891–1964)
George Gershwin	(1898–1937)
Richard Rodgers	(1902–1979)

Significant works by Jerome Kern, Cole Porter and George Gershwin are discussed below, while Richard Rodgers and Irving Berlin will feature in the next chapter.

Jerome Kern: *Show Boat*

Among the glut of musical plays that appeared in the 1920s, one can deservedly be called the first great musical. The music of *Show Boat* (1927) was composed by Jerome Kern to a book and lyrics by Oscar Hammerstein II, and was produced for Broadway by Florenz Ziegfeld. It was the first significant musical to be based on a novel – *Show Boat* by Edna Ferber, published the previous year.

Kern was a classically trained pianist who became a successful composer on tin-pan alley, contributing songs to numerous shows, including the *Ziegfeld Follies*. *Show Boat* stands out for the quality of its score, in which popular song plays an almost operatic role in developing an understanding of the characters. Some aspects of the libretto have been criticised (Hammerstein later came to regret contriving a happy ending to what is often a poignant drama), but there is no denying its theatrical daring in the hitherto cosy world of light-weight musical plays. It tells an epic story, spanning 47 years, of the lives of the multiracial group of people (owners, crew and entertainers) who worked on a Mississippi show boat called 'Cotton Blossom' – the vessel supplying a stunning visual backdrop for the production. It broaches subjects that no musical had ever tackled before, such as racism and the breakdown of marriage.

Kern's score reflects the passage of time by using a variety of styles, ranging from waltz-songs and actual quotations of popular 19th-century pieces, through ragtime and foxtrots to the blues-inflected 'Can't help lovin' dat man', one of several hit tunes embedded in the show:

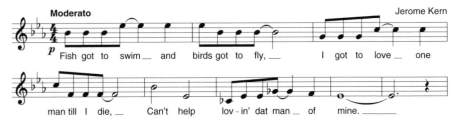

Typical of the dramatic intensity of *Show Boat* is the moment when this seemingly innocent love song is first sung by the apparently white Julie. Queenie, the ship's African-American cook warns that she 'didn't ever hear anybody but coloured folks sing dat song'. Kern's prominent flat 3rd on G♭ is a 'blue note' (from the blues) and is the musical cue that foreshadows Julie's later exposure as being of mixed race. Her marriage to a white man therefore contravened the state law of the day, which forbade mixed marriages, and they are forced to leave the show boat as a result.

Kern associates musical motifs with particular characters or ideas, and uses them to hint at what is to come in the drama or to remind the audience of what has happened. For example, the opening bars of Julie's song above were first heard much earlier in the show, played by the orchestra to accompany the cook's comic entrance. The audience is thus already subconsciously aware of the motif's extra-musical association long before Queenie makes it explicit.

The music of *Show Boat* is unified by numerous internal references of this sort. For example, characters particularly associated with the river (and the show boat itself) are linked by songs that emphasise repeated motifs which span the interval of a perfect 4th, as in the song quoted on page 30 and in the following three numbers:

There is an even closer link between the second and third of these songs – the opening of 'Ol' man river' is a rhythmic augmentation and free melodic inversion of the start of 'Cotton blossom'.

By using motifs in this way, Kern's music becomes an integral part of the drama, making unspoken connections and hinting at events to come. This technique is borrowed from grand opera, as Kern was well aware; he said that he wished 'to apply modern art to light music [as others] have done to more serious work'.

Equally operatic in ambition is the vocal range of many of the songs in *Show Boat* – far wider than that used in many other musicals of the day. For instance, 'Ol' man river' ascends from the low G quoted above to a top E, nearly two octaves higher – and the same singer needs to manage a succession of top Fs when the same song is reprised a semitone higher in Act 2.

Kern and Hammerstein were also prepared to break with tradition in other ways. For example, the tenor lead is unable to complete the final phrase of his first big song when he catches sight of the girl of his dreams. Instead of a conventional climactic ending followed by a break for applause, the two of them continue in **melodrama** (in this context 'melodrama' means spoken dialogue accompanied by music) – the music serves to push the action ahead rather than interrupt it. This is a work in which music plays a far more important role than the entertaining songs and dances that adorn earlier musical plays – hence *Show Boat's* claim to being the first modern musical.

Cole Porter: *Anything Goes* and *Kiss Me, Kate*

Cole Porter was the well-educated son of a wealthy and ambitious mother who had encouraged him to learn the violin and piano from an early age, and supported his childhood attempts at composition by paying for their publication. Porter's interest in songwriting developed while studying at Harvard and Yale universities, but it remained essentially a hobby until he decided to give up the study of law in order to write songs for Broadway revues in 1916. These were not a success, but with private financial means he was able to move to Paris, where he enjoyed partying with high society and developing a reputation as something of a wealthy playboy.

After returning to America, Porter first attracted attention with 'Let's fall in love', one of the songs he contributed to a 1928 Broadway revue, called *Paris*. Porter's witty lyrics and catchy melody perfectly reflected the frivolous spirit of the 1920s:

> Birds do it, bees do it,
> Even educated fleas do it,
> Let's do it, let's fall in love.

Later we learn that 'The dragonflies in the reeds do it, Sentimental centipedes do it' and that 'The chimpanzees in the zoos do it, Some courageous kangaroos do it'.

This is Porter's first example of a **list song** – a number with lyrics based on a list, often of increasing absurdity. The list song dates back to at least the 18th century (there is a famous 'catalogue aria' in Mozart's opera *Don Giovanni*) and was popular in 19th-century operetta (one of Gilbert and Sullivan's best-known examples is 'I have a little list' from *The Mikado*), but in the 20th century it was a genre that Cole Porter made very much his own.

A succession of musicals followed, mostly now forgotten apart from the memorable hit numbers they contained. These songs, all with lyrics as well as music by Cole Porter, include 'You do something to me' (1929), 'Love for sale' (1930) and 'Night and day' (1932).

Porter's *Anything Goes* (1934) had one of the longest runs of any Broadway musical in the 1930s, exceeded only by Gershwin's *Of Thee I Sing* (see page 40), and yet it seems extraordinary that it ever reached the stage at all. The idea came from Broadway producer Vinton Freedley, who had been virtually bankrupted by the great depression of the early 1930s. Taking a huge gamble, for he had no money, Freedley commissioned the book from two English writers, Guy Bolton (who had written for several early musical comedies on Broadway) and the famous humourist, P. G. Wodehouse. He engaged Ethel Merman, one of the most powerfully voiced and popular singers of the day for the leading role, and persuaded Cole Porter to write the score. With such a galaxy of names signed up, he was then able to secure the necessary finance.

But the book from Bolton and Wodehouse, provisionally entitled 'Hard to Get', was a disaster – even after a requested rewrite. Essentially, they struggled to elicit humour from their tale of a sinking ship. Two relatively inexperienced writers, Howard Lindsay and Russel Crouse, were hastily drafted in for a total rewrite, leaving very little of the original script intact but achieving the result that Freedley wanted – a musical farce of mistaken identity and improbable romance set onboard a luxury liner, not an epic drama in the style of *Show Boat*. Little of the revised script was ready by the time rehearsals started, and Ethel Merman had to use her secretarial training to jot down improvised additions in shorthand before typing them up for the cast to learn.

All of this left Porter only weeks to complete the songs. Not surprisingly, a number were replaced or altered immediately before, and even after, the opening night. The many revivals of *Anything Goes* over the years have continued to see numerous changes, particularly in the addition of famous songs from other Cole Porter musicals.

Despite – or perhaps because of – this creative pressure, *Anything Goes* contains some of Porter's best work. In place of the usual opening chorus, he began with one of the show's biggest hits, 'I get a kick out of you' – although he later followed Ethel Merman's advice to reprise it in Act 2 'for the benefit of those who had arrived late!' The frantic schedule is also said to have fortuitously given the show its eventual title when, at a late-night meeting, an exasperated member of the team demanded 'And just how the hell are we going to end the first act?', 'At this point,' replied one of the producers, 'anything goes!'. Whether this legend is true or not, Porter ended Act 1 with the show's exuberant title song, 'Anything goes':

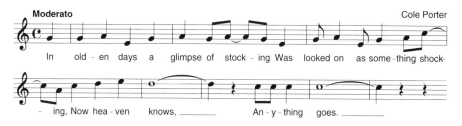

The pentatonicism of this first phrase from the 32-bar chorus contrasts vividly with the chromaticism of its bridge:

But the most characteristic feature of the entire song is its syncopation, particularly in the breathless riff-like repetitions of the bridge. These forceful rhythms are the trigger for a complex tap-dancing routine that forms part of this magnificent production number.

Among many other memorable numbers in *Anything Goes* are 'You're the top', which is another of Porter's famous list songs ('You're the Nile, You're the Tow'r of Pisa, You're the smile on the Mona Lisa …'), 'All through the night' – a love song with an unusual chorus almost entirely constructed from descending chromatic scales, 'Sailor's chantey' – Porter's modern interpretation of a sea shanty, and 'Blow, Gabriel, blow' – another big production number that has echoes of a fiery spiritual.

Such variety helped to ensure the show's success but also exposed its weakness. *Anything Goes* is essentially an old-style musical play, in which songs adorn the plot but rarely further the action, and in which the characters lack the three-dimensional depth of those in *Show Boat*. *Anything Goes* was essentially a showcase for the talents of Ethel Merman, for whom Porter wrote several more musicals over the next ten years. Like some of his earlier works, most of these shows are outlived by their hit songs, which include such standards as 'Begin the beguine', 'My heart belongs to daddy' and 'It's de-lovely'.

It was only after the 1943 production of Rodgers' and Hammerstein's *Oklahoma!* (see page 44) that Cole Porter explored the potential of the 'book musical'. The result was *Kiss Me, Kate* (1948), which was to be his longest-running success. The book, by Samuel and Bella Spewack, is based on Shakespeare's comedy *The Taming of the Shrew*, transposed into a modern context. Porter, as usual, wrote the lyrics as well as the music. *Kiss Me, Kate* retains the 'play within a play' device of its Elizabethan model. Two divorced actors, Fred and Lilli, find themselves performing opposite each other in the roles of Petruchio and Katherine (fiesty Kate, the 'shrew') in a musical adaptation of *The Taming of the Shrew*. The part of Bianca (Kate's sister) is played by Fred's current fancy, Lois, but she is far more interested in Bill, who is playing Lucentio.

The makings of great mischief is thus set up – the mutual loathing of Fred and Lilli, along with the complex off-stage love life of Lois and her two suitors, threatens to wreck the production. Into this scenario comes a pair of gangsters who have to collect a gambling debt from Bill. He convinces them that he will be able to pay up if they can only persuade Lilli not to storm out of the show – which involves the gangsters dressing-up to take part in the performance. Confusion descends to farce before the inevitable happy ending in which Fred and Lilli get back together, and Lois and Bill are finally married.

The book inspired some of Porter's best and most integrated work. He began

and other well-known numbers include 'Wunderbar' (a duet in waltz style), 'Brush up your Shakespeare', 'I hate men' (a vitriolic solo for Kate in Act 1) and, after the shrew has been 'tamed' in Act 2, a delicate setting of Shakespeare's own words from Kate's final (and somewhat sexist) speech in the original play, 'I am ashamed that women are so simple'. 'Brush up your Shakespeare' is a list song in the form of a comedy duet for the gangsters. which Porter cleverly introduced near the end of the show at the point where the audience might have expected to have already heard all the best tunes.

Porter's most modern song comes at the start of Act 2, when the stage crew of the 'play within a play' are taking a breather outside the theatre. The heavy jazz number 'Too darn hot' is dominated by a stonking two-bar riff with a blue flat 7th (D♮) that vividly captures the oppressive night-time temperature:

35

As the men boast of what they are going to do with their girls, the melody rises higher and higher – only to flop back to the riff at the end of each verse as they realise that 'it's too darn hot'. Porter extends this chorus straight into an increasingly exciting jazz dance routine, interrupted in the middle by the men chanting on a monotone 'Hot! Hot! Too hot!' – a moment uncannily like the shouts of 'Mambo! Mambo! Go!' to be heard nine years later in *West Side Story*'s 'Dance at the Gym'. After *Kiss Me, Kate*, the first show ever to win a 'Tony' award for the best Broadway musical, Cole Porter's later work achieved mixed success, and he eventually gave up composing, spending his final years in seclusion.

George Gershwin: *Porgy and Bess*

George Gershwin's early experience was as a plugger (a promoter of new songs) in tin-pan alley and as a rehearsal pianist for Broadway shows. In 1919 he wrote a song called 'Swanee', to words by Irving Caesar (later to be co-lyricist of *No, No, Nanette*) for an otherwise unmemorable Broadway revue. The next year it was recorded by Al Jolson, one of the most popular singers of the age, and it quickly became Gershwin's first major hit, selling over one million copies of the sheet music.

Unlike many of his contemporaries, Gershwin had a good grasp of jazz, which was becoming all the rage in the 1920s, and wrote several works, including *Rhapsody in Blue* (1924) and *An American in Paris* (1928), that imaginatively incorporated jazz-like ideas into music intended for the concert hall.

In the world of musicals, George Gershwin's most acclaimed works are the songs he wrote to lyrics by his brother Ira. Their Broadway collaborations include *Lady Be Good* (1924), *Funny Face* (1927) and *Girl Crazy* (1930), which includes the famous number 'I got rhythm'. Ira's lyrics were vital to Gershwin's success; he had an extraordinary gift for manipulating language to produce memorably modern phrases that inspired his brother's most elegant melodies, as in the following two songs from *Girl Crazy*:

'S wonderful! 'S marvelous!
You should care for me!

Embrace me, my sweet embraceable you.
Embrace me, you irreplaceable you.

Gershwin's ambition to develop the musical in new directions first surfaced in *Of Thee I Sing* (1931), the longest-running musical of the decade. It is rather like a Gilbert and Sullivan operetta for the jazz age – a biting political satire about presidential life in the White House, with some of the dialogue set as **recitative** (fast-moving vocal music with minimal accompaniment that follows the rhythms and patterns of speech) – see the example from *Porgy and Bess* on the next page.

Gershwin's 'folk opera' *Porgy and Bess* (1935) goes much further. He had originally envisaged a premiere at New York's Metropolitan Opera House. In the event it was launched on Broadway (carefully avoiding the word 'opera' in reference to the work) where it was easier to assemble the African-American cast that Gershwin wanted, but today it is more likely to be presented in an opera house than a theatre.

The work is based on the 1925 novel *Porgy* by DuBose Heyward, and its 1927 adaptation as a stage play by DuBose and his wife Dorothy. Both Heywards collaborated with the Gershwins on the book and lyrics for *Porgy and Bess*. It tells a story of social realism about Porgy, a crippled African-American living in the slums of Charleston in the south of the United States, and his attempts to rescue Bess from her pimp (named Crown) and the drug dealer known as Sportin' Life.

The work is through-composed, using recitative for the dialogue that occurs between the main musical numbers:

Gershwin insisted on the recitative, against the advice of DuBois Heyward, because it has the advantage of keeping the entire work within the single world of musical drama, avoiding the often awkward transition between speech and song when dialogue is spoken.

But his decision has been the subject of much controversy. A number of native speakers felt that Gershwin failed to capture the inflexions of African-American dialect, and the work's lukewarm reception and consequent financial failure were blamed partly on the fact that audiences were unfamiliar with the conventions of recitative. A revival on Broadway in 1942 replaced the recitatives with spoken dialogue, as well as making numerous cuts. However, in recent decades, most new productions (particularly by opera companies) have tended to respect the unity and integrity of Gershwin's original concept.

Equally operatic are the events that unfold in the plot of the musical. *Porgy and Bess* opens with an evocative picture of a sultry evening on Catfish Row, Charleston. An on-stage pianist is playing a slow blues to which couples dance and lazily croon 'Da-doo-wa'. Lighting highlights a different part of the stage, where Clara is singing a lullaby to her baby, which is the most famous song in the show, 'Summertime'. Gershwin perfectly captures the moment with a simple modal melody built around the descending minor 3rd that is a characteristic of the blues, but is underpinned by lush strings and richly chromatic harmony that evoke the mother's love and wealth of worldly experiences.

Porgy's entry is accompanied by a motif that features another blues-like descending minor 3rd (shown by a bracket in **A** below). We soon learn that this is a symbol of his loneliness – hinted at in his dismissal of women passing him by (**B** below) and then made explicit at the end of anguished phrase **C**:

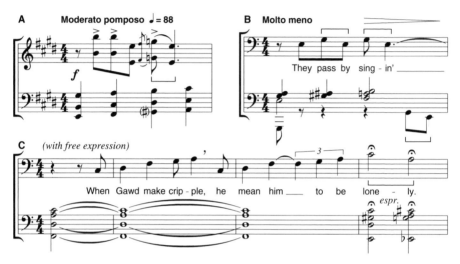

There are many similar examples of Gershwin's opera-like transformations of motifs in this way. For instance, when in the recitative shown on page 37, Bess indicates to Crown that Porgy will be lonely without her, she repeatedly uses the same pitches as motif **A**. Indeed, the final notes of the entire work, after Porgy has lost the only person he has ever loved, poignantly refer back to the loneliness of motif **A**.

Porgy's arrival signals the start of a gambling game with dice, which includes Crown and his woman Bess. In an elaborate contrapuntal ensemble, Gershwin builds up the tension towards the moment when Crown, having suffered heavy losses, murders one of the players in a drunken rage. Crown runs away before the police arrive, leaving Bess to fend for herself. Nobody will protect her – except Porgy. The remainder of the first act is dominated by scenes of mourning for the dead man, including the lament of his widow Serena, 'My man's gone now', based around the lonely minor 3rd motif, and the spiritual-like finale, 'Leavin' for the Promis' Lan''.

Act 2 sees a transformation in Porgy, now that he is living with Bess, expressed in the old-style banjo song 'I got plenty o' nuttin' – and nuttin's plenty for me'. The atmosphere is further lightened by a comedy routine in which Porgy instructs a phony lawyer to divorce Bess from the absent Crown, and ends up having to pay him extra because the pair were never married in the first place. Suddenly a buzzard flies low overhead – a premonition of evil for the superstitious – and Porgy catches Sportin' Life holding out the promise of riches in New York for Bess and offering her some of his 'happy dust'. Porgy sees him off and reassures her in the great love duet 'Bess, you is my woman now'.

The residents of Catfish Row go to a nearby island for a picnic; wild dancing begins with African drums and continues with ferocious $\frac{5}{4}$ rhythms. Then Sportin' Life sidles up to preach his cynical views on the Bible in another of the work's most famous songs, 'It ain't necessarily so':

The sinuous chromatic triplets perfectly convey the drug-dealer's snake-like character, while the bracketed interval is a tritone – an interval that has been known since medieval times as *diabolus in musica* (the devil in music).

As the crowd returns to Catfish Row, Bess is intercepted by Crown, who has been hiding on the island. She pleads to be allowed to return to Porgy, but Crown forces her to stay with him in the woods.

A week has passed, and Bess is back with Porgy, having been lost for two days. She is delirious and her cries of 'take your hands off me' hint at what has happened. Serena prays for her recovery in 'Oh, doctor Jesus', an atmospheric incantation sung over eerily trilling pedal notes. The calls of street-sellers hawking strawberries and crabs are heard from outside, and Bess slowly returns to normality. She tells Porgy she loves him, despite what has happened, and he promises to protect her from Crown. Just then, a terrible storm blows up and the fearful tolling of the hurricane bell is heard; Clara's husband and the other men are out at sea fishing.

The people of Catfish Row pray for deliverance in a complex contrapuntal version of 'Oh, doctor Jesus'. They think they hear death knocking on the door as the storm rages, but it flies open to reveal Crown, who has come for Bess. Clara suddenly sees her husband's boat, floating upside down and rushes out to save him with the aid of Crown, who taunts Porgy's physical inability to help. The entire scene is coloured by the dramatic contrast between the spiritual-like prayers for mercy and the tempestuous action, ending with a return of 'Oh, doctor Jesus'.

The third act begins with the revelation that both Clara and her husband have perished in the storm. Bess is left singing 'Summertime' to their orphaned baby. However, Crown has survived and is seen in the shadows, heading for Porgy's door. As he passes the window, a hand grasping a long knife appears. It belongs to Porgy who, murderously triumphing over his disability, stabs Crown in the back with the cry of 'Bess, Bess, you got a *man* now, you got Porgy!'.

The police arrive to investigate the death and ask Porgy to identify the body. Porgy refuses, having been spooked by Sportin' Life into believing that a corpse will bleed in the presence of its murderer. Porgy is arrested for contempt of court and Sportin' Life convinces Bess that she will never see Porgy again and that the pair of them should run away to New York. Although she tries to rebuff him and his happy dust, he leaves a packet on the step, ironically singing 'All right I'll leave it here' to the melody of 'It ain't necessarily so'.

One week later, Porgy is out of jail and in buoyant mood. He has bought presents for Bess and his friends and cannot understand why they seem so downhearted or why Serena is now looking after the baby. He sings the emotional ballad 'Bess, oh where's my Bess?' and the others reply that 'She gone back to de happy dus'' and tell him that she has run off with Sportin' Life. In a moment of utmost poignancy, the final curtain falls on Porgy singing 'Oh Lawd, I'm on my way' as he gets into his tiny goat cart for the impossible thousand-mile trek to find the only person he ever loved.

Perhaps such operatic tragedy was too much for a musical. The original production ran for only 124 performances (compared with the 441 performances of Gershwin's now seldom-heard *Of Thee I Sing* a few years earlier) and was subjected to considerable criticism for its negative portrayal of African-Americans as people with low self-esteem, stereotyped as drug dealers and pimps. It is possible that Gershwin's high-minded preoccupation with creating a new type of work by fusing classical and jazz techniques with blues and folk-like material, diverted his attention from a range of more basic issues – including whether such essentially simple material is enhanced by this type of treatment and, even more fundamentally, why Gershwin should presume he had the authority to speak on behalf of black America in his 'folk opera'.

Time has resulted in a more considered appreciation of *Porgy and Bess* as a brilliant snapshot of its age. But Gershwin was to write nothing more for Broadway before his death from a brain tumour in 1937, less than two years after the opening night; his final months were spent writing for the new medium of musical films.

Musical films

The development of techniques to synchronise recorded sound with film saw silent pictures quickly giving way to the new 'talking movies' by the end of the 1920s. One of the earliest was *The Jazz Singer* (1927) which, although still mainly silent (with words shown on 'title cards'), has a soundtrack for some scenes. Despite the fact that there are several songs earlier in the film, *The Jazz Singer* is always remembered for the first words spoken by Al Jolson to introduce his performance of Irving Berlin's song 'Blue skies', which has become one of the most famous lines in the history of film: 'Wait a minute! Wait a minute! You ain't heard nothing yet!'

The Jazz Singer is not a musical – the songs, which came from a variety of sources, are purely incidental to the plot. The first film musical proper was *The Broadway Melody*, which appeared in 1929. Although hugely successful, it is remembered particularly for its technical achievements, which included a sequence shot in colour and the use of sound editing and pre-recording of some of the soundtrack. The latter arose when it was decided to re-shoot an elaborate scene and the sound engineer suggested that the soundtrack, which was fine, could be reused. Filming without the presence of live musicians and microphones meant that the noisy cameras of the day no longer had to work from within soundproof boxes, enabling directors to explore much more interesting camera angles. Equally, recording the music in advance, away from the electrical interference of film lights and the cluttered spaces of a film set resulted in much better sound quality. This method quickly became standard for the succession of musical films that rapidly followed.

These included film versions of recent stage musicals such as Romberg's *The Desert Song* (1929) and Friml's *The Vagabond King* (1930), as well as new works written specifically for the cinema, such as Hammerstein and Romberg's *Viennese Nights* (1930). All of these were shot in colour, a medium that the public increasingly came to associate with musical films.

One of the key figures in cinema of the 1930s was the choreographer and director Busby Berkeley. Dance numbers in early musical films had been little different to performances on a stage, and would be filmed from one or two fixed camera positions. Berkeley saw the potential for film to develop something much more spectacular and devised lavish production numbers in which large numbers of showgirls would dance in dazzling geometric patterns. He mounted cameras on tracks to get sweeping views of them, and on cranes to get kaleidoscopic overhead shots, creating perspectives that would be impossible to achieve in a theatrical show.

Although taste for Berkeley's precise but predictable routines soon waned, it led to an interest in the musical film as a vehicle for dance, seen particularly in the series of light romantic comedy films starring the dancers Fred Astaire and Ginger Rogers. Most famous was *Top Hat* (1935) with songs by Irving Berlin that included such hit numbers as 'I'm puttin' on my top hat' and 'Dancing cheek to cheek'.

Musical films attracted, and furthered the careers of, many other notable stars of the day. In 1942, Bing Crosby (along with Fred Astaire) starred in *Holiday Inn*, the most successful film musical to date. Again it featured songs by Berlin, including 'Sisters' and that perennial favourite 'I'm dreaming of a white Christmas'. In 1939, the 16-year-old Judy Garland landed the role of Dorothy in *The Wizard of Oz*, a musical based on a children's novel of 1900 by L. Frank Baum. The songs composed by Harold Arlen (to lyrics by E. Y. Harburg) include 'Over the rainbow', one of the most well-known popular songs of all time.

'Over the rainbow' was nearly cut from the film, because it slowed the pace of the action, but associate producer Arthur Freed is said to have rescued it. Freed subsequently headed a unit that produced a succession of musical films for MGM, including *Meet Me in St. Louis* (1944) with three new hit songs for Judy Garland by Hugh Martin and Ralph Blane – 'The boy next door', 'The trolley song' and 'Have yourself a merry little Christmas'. *Easter Parade* (1948) starred Bing Crosby alongside Judy Garland performing songs by Irving Berlin. A film version of Bernstein's early stage musical *On the Town* followed in 1949, while *An American in Paris* (1951) was a showcase for the dancing skills of Gene Kelly. It is based on a selection of music by George Gershwin, who had died in 1937, and is thus an early example of a compilation musical. It includes an 18-minute dance sequence, set to Gershwin's symphonic poem *An American in Paris*.

Freed followed it up with another compilation musical starring Gene Kelly, *Singin' in the Rain* (1952). For this work, most of the songs came from earlier MGM musicals in which Freed himself had been the lyricist and Nacio Herb Brown the composer. The title song, during which Kelly performs one of his most spectacular dance routines, was taken from one of the earliest musical films, *The Hollywood Revue of 1929*.

Freed's final success, signalling the end of the MGM musical, was *Gigi* (1958). Written by Alan Lerner and Frederick Loewe, the team responsible for *My Fair Lady* (see page 49), it maintained the tradition of including a succession of hit songs, including 'Thank heaven for little girls' and 'The night they invented champagne'. But, despite their success, such songs seemed very old-fashioned in the rock-and-roll years of the late 1950s – a time that also saw the rise in popularity of television and consequent sharp decline in cinema attendance. Musical film was no longer an important vehicle for getting the latest hit songs to the market and the rapidly changing styles of new pop music were not well-suited to the long production schedules of film-making.

Many film musicals after 1960 have been cinematic adaptations of existing stage shows, so will be mentioned in later chapters in conjunction with their theatrical originals. Film musicals have declined in the face of films that primarily use music as a promotional tool, either including pop or rock tracks as background music, or featuring a big tune to help sell the film, such as James Horner's song 'My heart will go on', included, with some misgivings by its director, in the film *Titanic* (1997).

There are however two important exceptions to this decline. One is the increasingly successful Bollywood film industry, which maintains the tradition of many western musicals in its use of escapist light-romantic plots, star performers in brilliant costumes, vivid scenery, spectacular production numbers with set-piece dances, and a succession of popular songs. All of this is fused into a unique blend of western and Indian musical styles.

The other is the type of feature-length animated film, particularly from the Disney studio, aimed primarily at children (although often popular with a wider audience). Most of these films have a strong musical element, including tuneful songs that are integrated into the plot and written in a traditional popular style.

The first of such works – and, indeed, the first successful full-length animated film – was Disney's *Snow White and the Seven Dwarfs* (1937). Its succession of memorable tunes, composed by Frank Churchill (a Disney staff composer who had worked on earlier short animations), range from the beautiful aspirational ballad 'Some day my prince will come' to the buoyant 'Whistle while you work' and 'Heigh-ho'.

Fantasia (1940) has a soundtrack of classical orchestral excerpts, each interpreted in a series of stunningly-choreographed animations. Although now regarded as one of Disney's most original works, its experimental nature was not well received at the time, and he returned to animated films based on conventional stories with music that usually delivered at least one big hit tune – such as the inspirational ballad 'When you wish upon a star' from *Pinocchio* (1940) or the sing-along 'Zip-a-dee-doo-dah' from *Song of the South* (1946).

Many of Disney's later animations, such as *Lady and the Tramp* and *101 Dalmations*, are remembered more for their dramatic and visual impact than their music, but a new direction was signaled in 1964 with the release of *Mary Poppins*, based on the children's books by P. L. Travers. It was Disney's first musical to be based primarily on live action, enhanced by animated sequences. The score by brothers Robert B. Sherman and Richard M. Sherman (sons of a former tin-pan alley composer) included such numbers as 'A spoonful of sugar', 'Supercalifragilisticexpialidocious' and the nostalgic 'Chim Chim Cher-ee'. A highly successful stage musical version of *Mary Poppins*, based on the film, opened in 2004. The Shermans went on to write scores for many later musical films, including Disney's feature-length animation *Jungle Book* (1967), which includes the popular 'Bare necessities' and 'I wanna be like you'.

After some rather lean years, the Disney studios again achieved hits with *The Little Mermaid* (1989) and *Beauty and the Beast* (1991) – both with lyrics by Howard Ashman and music by Alan Menken, the team that had achieved success back in 1982 with *Little Shop of Horrors* (see page 66). For the songs of *Lion King* (1994, see page 75), Disney studios turned to lyricist Tim Rice, composer Elton John and the South-African musician, Lebo M. In 1997 the film of *Lion King* was adapted to form what has now become a long-running stage musical.

THE HENLEY COLLEGE LIBRARY

4

The golden age

Rodgers and Hammerstein: *Oklahoma!*

Although linking the names of Rodgers and Hammerstein seems as familiar today as the pairing of Gilbert and Sullivan, the composer Richard Rodgers and the librettist Oscar Hammerstein II had each established successful independent careers on Broadway before working together on *Oklahoma!* (1943).

Rodgers' first writing partner was the lyricist Lorenz Hart, whom he met while they were students at Columbia University, New York. Rodgers and Hart wrote 29 stage musicals together, including the popular *On Your Toes* (1936) and *Pal Joey* (1940), both featuring a strong element of dance. In the 1940s Lorenz Hart began to suffer from alcohol-related problems and died in 1943 at the early age of 48.

Meanwhile, Hammerstein (who had also attended Columbia University, where he had worked briefly with Rodgers and Hart) had contributed to numerous musical shows including works by Youmans, Friml and Romberg. One of his most significant early successes was writing the book and lyrics for Jerome Kern's *Show Boat*.

In 1942 Rodgers was unable to persuade Hart to start on a new project, a musical based on Lynn Riggs' play *Green Grow the Lilacs*, that would eventually be entitled *Oklahoma!*, so he turned to his old student friend, Oscar Hammerstein II, who had independently had the same idea, but couldn't persuade Jerome Kern to write the music. Thus began the most famous partnership in the history of the musical.

To fully understand the impact made by *Oklahoma!* in 1943, it is important to realise that the public's expectations of musicals had been shaped by earlier musical comedies such as *No, No, Nanette* and *Anything Goes* (and musical films like *Holiday Inn*) in which short songs adorn an amusing play – integrated dramas such as *Porgy and Bess* and *Show Boat* were not typical of the 1930s musical. *Oklahoma!* was something fresh – a work containing extended musical numbers in which song and dance play an essential role in the drama, furthering the action and serving to develop the audience's understanding of the characters and their motivation.

The work is set in America's Indian Territory, shortly before it became the state of Oklahoma in 1907, when farmers and cattle ranchers were competing for land and water rights. It centres on the rivalry between a cowboy named Curly and a hired hand named Jud, both in love with Laurey, a farm girl. A comic subplot is provided by another love triangle – the cowboy Will Parker is in love with Ado Annie, who can't say no to any man, having a particular weakness for the travelling salesman Ali Hakim.

Oklahoma! begins with the customary potpourri overture, but thereafter is anything but conventional. Instead of an opening chorus, the curtain rises to the sound of Curly, initially heard off-stage and unaccompanied, singing the show's first big hit number while he strolls onto the set. 'Oh, what a beautiful morning' is a perfectly balanced waltz-song in **verse-and-chorus form**, in which 16-bar verses alternate with 16-bar choruses. The former are based on stepwise melodic movement and elegantly complement the triadic shapes of the chorus:

Hammerstein's words fit Rodgers' melody like a glove. His technique of reiterating the essence of the lyric in the first three lines ('beautiful morning', 'beautiful day', 'beautiful feeling') is faithfully reflected by Rodgers' use of three phrases with identical starts (falling then rising triads) but different endings. Similarly, just as Hammerstein's fourth line differs in suggesting an outcome ('Everything's going my way'), so Rodgers' fourth phrase differs in starting with *two* falling triadic patterns. The song as a whole establishes the scene of gloriously sunny farmland and buoyant optimism, the 'American dream' in fact, that dominates the work and that so appealed to audiences in war-torn 1943.

Laurey enters singing a snatch of Curly's song. Although she feigns no interest in going to a dance with him, the music has already planted a connection between them in the minds of the audience. Curly gets her to imagine what it would be like to turn up in style in 'The Surrey with a fringe on top' – a novelty song with a rhythm to depict the sound of the horse's hooves pulling the type of carriage known as a Surrey. The stubborn Laurey dismisses the idea as make-believe.

After a scene in which Will Parker and the other cowboys tell of their trip to Kansas City and demonstrate the latest dances they have picked up, Curly learns that Laurey is going to the dance with the surly Jud Fry. It turns out that the Surrey was not imaginary – Curly had hired it especially to impress Laurey. The events trigger a reprise of 'The Surrey with a fringe on top', but now subdued and almost bitter – thus giving the conventional device of a reprise a real function of its own in the drama. Another girl volunteers to go to the dance with Curly –

Laurey, stubborn as ever, pretends she doesn't care a jot: 'Many a new face will please my eye, Many a new love will find me'. Meanwhile, comic relief is provided by Ado Annie, who can't decide whether to go to the dance with Will Parker or Ali Hakim. The trouble is, she sings, 'I'm jist a girl who cain't say no'.

Curly tells Laurey that everyone was expecting him to take her to the dance. In the duet 'People will say we're in love', the couple maintain the charade of saying exactly the opposite of what they really mean: 'Don't throw bouquets at me … Don't sigh and gaze at me'. Curly decides to confront Jud and taunts him with a vision of mourners around his coffin in the mock funeral march 'Poor Jud is daid'. Jud, polishing his gun, darkly warns that Curly may die first. Later, Jud is alone and reveals more of his character in 'Lonely Room', a song of narrow range and dissonant accompaniment reflecting Jud's disturbed character.

Laurey is confused by her feelings for Curly but her friends know what she is thinking: 'Out of your dreams and into his arms you long to be'. She falls asleep and a long ballet sequence begins in which dancers, personifying Laurey, Curly and their friends, enact the happy wedding of the couple. As 'Laurey' lifts her veil at the altar, the dream turns to nightmare – it is 'Jud' standing beside her. 'Curly' attacks him, but 'Jud' chokes him to death and carries 'Laurey' away. At that point the real Jud wakes the sleeping Laurey and takes her off to the dance, leaving Curley alone and dejected as the curtain falls.

The 15-minute dream sequence provides an extraordinary contrast to the usual type of Act 1 finale heard in musicals, with its upbeat singing and jolly dancing. Here, ballet is used as a key part of the drama, providing a new and unexpected insight into Laurey's troubled emotional state.

Act 2 begins with a lively barn dance, 'The farmer and the cowman should be friends', that serves a triple purpose: it begins the social dance that has been the cause of all the conflict in Act 1, it lightens the atmosphere by providing a perfect foil for the formal ballet before the interval, and it hints at a resolution of conflict between the farming and ranching communities that will form the focus of the finale.

The girls have prepared picnic hampers for a fund-raising auction at the dance. Will Parker outbids Ali Hakim for Ado Annie's basket and eventually gets her to decide (in his favour) between her two suitors. But the auction for Laurey's basket is altogether more serious. Curly and Jud each bid everything they have, while the crowd nervously sings a reminder that 'The farmer and the cowman should be friends'. Curly manages to win the bidding war by selling his gun and at last plucks up the courage to kiss Laurey, who finally admits that she is terrified by Jud and has fired him as a farm hand. It's the cue for another meaningful reprise – 'People will say we're in love' is heard again for the first time since the middle of Act 1 but now, at last, both partners are being true to their feelings and the lyrics change to '*Let* people say we're in love'.

Three weeks later, the wedding of Curly and Laurey is linked to the optimism of the creation of a brand new state – 'Oklahoma where the wind comes sweepin' down the plain' – and where the differences between ranchers and farmers have at last been resolved. But there is a sting in the tail after this very late appearance of the show's stunning title song. Just before the happy couple leave on their honeymoon, a drunken Jud arrives with a 'present' for the groom. It seems as if the premonition of the 'dream sequence' is about to come true – he strikes Curly and then draws a knife but, in a reversal of fortune, Curly throws him off and Jud lands on his own knife. Despite the late hour, everyone agrees that Curly is not to blame and, as the sun rises on another glorious Oklahoma day, the strains of 'Oh, what a glorious morning' see Curly and Laura at last getting on board the Surrey to leave for their honeymoon.

Oklahoma! was an ambitious musical that was new in many respects. It has:

- Extended musical numbers in which song often leads straight into dance or melodrama to develop the mood
- Dance that either arises logically from the plot, as in the barn dance, or that serves to go beyond words, as in the dream sequence
- Carefully-drawn three-dimensional characters (most of the first act is more about establishing character than furthering action)
- A witty book and lyrics written in a natural, conversational style
- An amusing sub-plot containing a secondary love story
- Music that presents a succession of memorable numbers as an integral part of the drama, and in which conventions such as the reprise are used to serve a dramatic purpose.

Audiences loved the musical, evidenced by the fact that the opening run lasted for well over 2,000 performances before going on tour for ten years, and the show was made into a film musical in 1955. Rodgers and Hammerstein had four more great successes with the following musicals:

- *Carousel* (1945), containing the famous number 'You'll never walk alone', which is often described as an **anthemic song** – an aspirational song that has become an anthem of loyalty for a particular group of people, such as football supporters.
- *South Pacific* (1949), particularly remembered for the song, 'Some enchanted evening'
- *The King and I* (1951), which includes the songs 'I whistle a happy tune' and 'Hello young lovers'
- *The Sound of Music* (1959), which contains a string of memorable numbers, including 'My favourite things', 'Do-re-mi', 'Sixteen going on seventeen', 'Edelweiss' and the anthemic 'Climb every mountain'.

After Hammerstein's death in 1960, Rodgers continued to write musicals until his own death in 1979, including *Do I Hear a Waltz?* (1965) with lyrics by Stephen Sondheim (Hammerstein's student). But none ever achieved the success of his works written in partnership with Oscar Hammerstein II.

Irving Berlin: *Annie Get Your Gun*

Following the success of *Oklahoma!*, other composers were quick to adopt the style of the book musical, in which music is designed to integrate completely with the plot. For example, Cole Porter's change of approach in *Kiss Me, Kate* (1948) has already been mentioned (see page 34).

Irving Berlin was a tin-pan alley composer whose first big hit song, *Alexander's Ragtime Band*, appeared in 1911. Much of his early work for the stage consisted of music for revues. One from 1917 included the song 'God bless America', which has become an unofficial alternative national anthem for the United States. As previously noted, Berlin was also successful in the field of musical films, including *Top Hat* (1935) and *Holiday Inn* (1942). But it was not until 1946 that he wrote the music and lyrics for a really successful stage musical – *Annie Get Your Gun*, which was produced by Rodgers and Hammerstein. The book, by the brother and sister team of Herbert and Dorothy Fields, is loosely based on the life of the sharp-shooting Annie Oakley, and Irving's music follows the example of *Oklahoma!* in that it uses song to define character and develop the plot.

The Fields had originally written the book for composer Jerome Kern, and only turned to Irving Berlin after Kern's unexpected death in 1945. Berlin was not sure he was up to the task, but within three days of receiving the script came up with both lyrics and music for three of the show's hit songs. These included the famous production number, 'There's no business like show business', sung after tom-boy Annie's success in a shooting contest results in her being asked to join a travelling wild west show. She falls in love with the star of the show, Frank, but he walks out when Annie's fame eclipses his own. After various complications they re-unite, still happily sparring in the syncopated comedy duet, 'Anything you can do, I can do better':

Book musicals dominated the 1950s, with shows such as Irving Berlin's *Call Me Madam* (1950) and Frank Loesser's *Guys and Dolls* (also 1950). The latter included the famous songs 'Luck be a lady' and 'Sit down, you're rockin' the boat'. But one musical was destined to become even more popular than *Oklahoma!*

Lerner and Loewe: *My Fair Lady*

Composer Frederick Loewe trained as a concert pianist in Vienna before coming to America with his parents in 1924. He began writing for the theatre in the 1930s, but did not achieve success until he teamed up with lyricist/librettist Alan Jay Lerner. After a couple of early flops their first two successful musicals were *Brigadoon* (1947) and *Paint Your Wagon* (1951).

For years George Bernard Shaw had refused requests to create a musical from his play, *Pygmalion*. It was only after Shaw's death in 1950 that it became a realistic prospect, but even Rodgers and Hammerstein, who worked on the idea themselves for over a year, thought the task was impossible.

Lerner and Loewe succeeded by basing *My Fair Lady* (1956) on Shaw's own screenplay for a 1938 film of *Pygmalion*, for which they had been able to clear the rights in 1954. For this, Shaw had added a ballroom scene (ideal to develop into a production number) and had also unwillingly allowed the work to end with a suggestion that the two main characters (Eliza Doolittle and her much older mentor, Professor Higgins) may have formed a romantic attachment. The latter was essential to the success of the musical, in which the stern bachelor Higgins eventually admits, with poignant understatement, that he'd 'grown accustomed to her face'.

In other respects, Lerner retained much of Shaw's brilliant dialogue, adding an opportunity for another production number (the Ascot scene), and developing the character of Alfred Doolittle, Eliza's father, in order to establish a comic sub-plot.

My Fair Lady is set in Edwardian London and centres on the boast of Higgins, an arrogant professor of phonetics, that he can train any woman to speak so well that she could mix unnoticed in high society. His friend Colonel Pickering wagers that he can't, and so Higgins sets out to prove Pickering wrong.

Following the overture, Act 1 opens in Covent Garden where Higgins is making notes on English dialects ('Why can't the English learn to speak?'). He is struck by the cockney dialect of a flower seller, Eliza Doolittle, and tells her that he and Pickering can teach her to better herself by speaking like a lady. Eliza is tempted, as she admits in 'Wouldn't it be loverly', a classic example of AABA song form (with an extended final A section). The beginning is shown on the next page.

All I want is a room some - where, Far a - way from the cold night air,

Eliza's father, Alfred, is a dustman and has spent all his wages on drink, but manages to get some cash out of his long-suffering daughter. In 'With a little bit of luck', Alfred and his friends expound their philosophy of life: 'A man was made to help support his children – but with a little bit o' luck, they'll go out and start supporting you'.

The next day Eliza arrives at Higgins' home for elocution lessons but they soon find each other mutually exasperating. In 'I'm an ordinary man', Higgins concludes that he will never let a woman in his life, while Eliza, driven to distraction by his thoughtless behaviour and endless speech exercises, retorts with 'Just you wait, 'Enry 'Iggins, just you wait!'

Eventually, though, Eliza learns to speak with an upper-class accent, and she and the professor celebrate in the tango-rhythm duet 'The rain in Spain falls mainly on the plain'. Eliza is too excited to sleep and imagines herself at the ball in 'I could have danced all night'.

Higgins decides to risk introducing Eliza to society at the Ascot Races. There she attracts the attention of Freddy Eynsford-Hill, who was first seen at the start of the musical, when he knocked over Eliza's flowers in Covent Garden. In conversation with Freddy and his mother, Eliza reveals that although she has learnt correct pronunciation she has not mastered polite conversation. She lets slip various slang expressions and ends up shocking everyone when she yells out to her horse 'Come on, Dover, move your bloomin' arse!'. Freddy, though, is smitten and later goes to Higgins' house hoping for just a glimpse of Eliza ('On the street where you live').

After more work, Eliza is ready for the embassy ball where she succeeds brilliantly, dancing with Higgins in the 'Embassy Waltz'. Afterwards, Eliza nostalgically recalls the pleasure of the evening in a reprise of 'I could have danced all night', but is distraught to discover that Higgins and Pickering have no time for her now their experiment is over. She throws Higgins' slippers at him and rushes from the house. Outside she stumbles into Freddy, who professes his love – but Eliza is sick of mere words and demands 'Show me!'.

Meanwhile, Alfred Doolittle has come into some money, thanks to an off-the-cuff remark by Higgins, and has decided to marry the woman he has been living with for years ('I'm getting married in the morning'). First, he spends one more night on the town, imploring his friends to 'Get me to the church on time'.

The clueless Higgins is puzzled by Eliza's apparent ingratitude and asks Pickering 'Why can't a woman be more like a man?' He goes to find her, but is still too stubborn to admit to his true feelings and ends the song 'Without you' with the line 'So go back in your shell, I can do bloody well without you!' But as he returns home he at last confesses that he's 'grown accustomed to her face'. Sitting alone at dusk, he is fondly playing a recording of Eliza's voice when she quietly enters the room. 'Liza!', the irascible professor exclaims as the curtain falls, 'Where the devil are my slippers?'

The show was a staggering success on Broadway. The leading roles were taken by three English actors, avoiding the problem of Americans trying to imitate British accents. Higgins was played by Rex Harrison who, being unable to sing, developed a unique style of reciting lyrics in a sort of 'speech-song' that merely approximated the correct pitches – something that Loewe took into account when writing Higgins' songs. Eliza was played by the young Julie Andrews, who would go on to star in the 1964 film musical *Mary Poppins* and the 1965 film version of *The Sound of Music*. Her father, Alfred, was played by the cockney comedian and character actor, Stanley Holloway. In addition, *My Fair Lady* had stunning period costumes designed by the queen's dressmaker, Cecil Beaton. A film version of the musical (including Rex Harrison and Stanley Holloway from the original stage musical) appeared in 1964 and the work has been revived many times since then.

Leonard Bernstein: *West Side Story*

Only one year after *My Fair Lady* had confirmed that the traditional musical was still alive and well, something altogether more challenging appeared in the shape of *West Side Story* (1957).

Leonard Bernstein was a multi-talented musician who established a reputation as a pianist, conductor, broadcaster and composer. In the last of these areas he followed in Gershwin's footsteps, often working at the frontier between popular and art music. But Bernstein's music reflects the popular styles of a later age – especially bebop jazz, with its hard-edged dissonance, Afro-Cuban jazz, with its Latin-American rhythms, and the urban blues. Bernstein was also influenced by the musicals of Kurt Weill, a German composer who moved to America and who, like Gershwin and Bernstein, drew on both popular and classical traditions in his music. Weill's best-known song is 'Mack the Knife' which comes from his 1928 musical play *Die Dreigroschenoper* ('The Threepenny Opera'), a reworking of John Gay's *The Beggar's Opera* in a jazz-based 20th-century style, written in collaboration with the German dramatist Bertolt Brecht. Bernstein had conducted the first concert performance of a new English translation of the work in 1952.

Bernstein had an early hit with the musical *On the Town* (1944), a work with a strong element of dance. A film version, which was considerably different from the original, appeared in 1949, produced by Arthur Freed and starring Gene Kelly and Frank Sinatra. Bernstein also wrote the score for the film *On the Waterfront* (1954), which is a direct predecessor of *West Side Story*, both musically and dramatically, as it too deals with harsh inner-city tensions, human conflict and social realism.

The idea of a musical based on Shakespeare's play *Romeo and Juliet* was suggested to Bernstein by the choreographer Jerome Robbins in 1949, the year after Porter's *Kiss Me, Kate* had shown how a Shakespearean plot could form the basis of a successful musical. The setting was changed from renaissance Italy to modern-day New York. Romeo and Juliet, the young lovers who defy a long-running feud between their families, become Tony and Maria from rival teenage gangs, the Jets and the Sharks. Shakespeare's famous balcony scene is mirrored by the meeting of Tony and Maria on the fire escape of a bleak New York tenement.

Some early sketches were made in 1949, but it was not until 1956 that Bernstein began work in earnest on the project. The screen-writer Arthur Laurents was engaged to write the book and Stephen Sondheim was asked to provide the lyrics. Sondheim was a student and friend of Oscar Hammerstein II and later became a composer of musicals in his own right. Robbins had envisaged that the conflict of loyalties, which is so central to the drama, could be interpreted as a conflict between Catholic and Jewish communities. Bernstein seized on the idea that current racial tensions in New York caused by a large influx of immigrants from Puerto Rico would provide a more powerful scenario – and he undoubtedly saw that this would also offer him the opportunity to use a range of Latin-American dance rhythms, for he later said:

> 'Suddenly it all sprang to life. I heard rhythms and pulses, and – most of all – I could sort of feel the form.'

Much about *West Side Story* was revolutionary. Instead of the nostalgic romanticism of earlier musicals, this is a story of bleak despair. Extended dance sequences convey the drama, and in place of rousing finales, both acts end in murder. Although Shakespeare's text is not used, his characters are clearly identifiable:

Romeo and Juliet	West Side Story
The Montague family	The Jets (Americans)
Mercutio (Montague's nephew)	Riff (their leader)
Romeo (Montague's son)	Tony (Riff's friend)
The Capulet family	The Sharks (Puerto Ricans)
Tybalt (Capulet's nephew)	Bernardo (their leader)
Juliet (Capulet's daughter)	Maria (Bernardo's sister)
Nurse	Anita (Bernardo's girlfriend)
Friar Laurence	Doc

Bernstein originally envisaged starting the work in a conventional way with an overture and opening chorus, but instead he decided on a much more dramatic solution. The curtain rises immediately on a long prologue in which action and tension are conveyed in dance, mime and music without words. The Jets are in control of the city streets and they are 'cool' – an expression that in the 1950s referred to a calculated display of controlled energy.

Arrogant finger-snaps (notated in the score) introduce a slinky saxophone phrase that ends with an interval, marked with a bracket (in example (a) below) that will come to dominate the work. It is a tritone, a traditional symbol of evil (see page 39) and it sets the scene for the ruthless violence of the Jets and Sharks.

Riffs, cross-rhythms, bitonality and textures made from layering independent parts are all hallmarks of Bernstein's style and are used to build dramatic tension for the entry of Bernardo, leader of the Sharks. This is signalled by the motif in example (b) below played on muted trombone, in which the tritone (bracketed) is written as an augmented 4th rather than a diminished 5th. Bernardo is taunted by two of the Jets, to another characteristic Bernstein sound – a solo break for drums of different pitches.

The tritone doesn't merely provide musical glue; it also has a clear dramatic purpose. For instance, in bars 108–109 example (b) is heard in shorter note values, as shown in example (c) below. This **pp** version in bare octaves underlines the baiting going on between the rival gangs. And when a Shark deliberately trips up a Jet, and thereby sets in motion the train of events that will lead to the final tragedy, we hear a curiously tripping figure, shown in example (d) below, in which tritones appear twice in succession, splitting the octave into two equal-sized intervals:

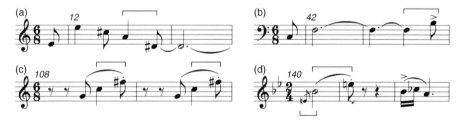

Bernstein builds the tension of this confrontational opening scene over a long period, often dropping back from intermediate climaxes by thinning the texture and reducing the dynamic, in order to give space for the next build-up. But the underlying quickening of intensity eventually leads to a searing semitonal dissonance when Bernardo attacks one of the Jets, and then to chaotic **fff** cross-rhythms as free-for-all fighting breaks out. A police whistle (notated in the score) is heard and there is time for only six more bars of fighting. When the police appear they are greeted by a sudden pretence of dreary normality: 'What's up? Nothing's wrong', the music seems to say, as the prologue ends with a nonchalant repeat of its first main melody.

Bernstein's opening faithfully reflects the drama, despite the absence of words, and the gradual transition to vocal music is equally skilful. The second number ('Jet song') begins with motifs from the prologue played under spoken dialogue. When Riff breaks into song, the accompaniment is based on a syncopated $\frac{6}{8}$ pattern heard at the start of the musical and that has already been associated with the Jets. But above this Bernstein writes a vocal part in crotchets, effectively in $\frac{3}{4}$ time. The forceful cross-rhythms, angular melody and entirely syllabic setting give enormous weight to Riff's authoritarian statement as gang leader: 'When you're a Jet, you're a Jet all the way'. The middle section of the verse develops the saxophone melody from the prologue example (a) above. Its disjunct motion and prominent tritone, along with dissonant chord clusters in the accompaniment, leave no doubt that Riff is a hard man.

Riff's best friend, Tony, is growing disillusioned with the Jets. His first song ('Something's coming') anticipates the excitement of the dance to be held that night at the gym and also reveals his desire for a different and better future. The urgency is conveyed by a driving tempo and short riffs that permeate the accompaniment – the ever-present tritone appears both melodically and harmonically.

A short scene of spoken dialogue introduces Maria and Anita, who work in a bridal shop. As it ends Maria imagines the dance to be held that night and whirls across the stage in the dress she has made for the occasion. As she does so, a spectacular stage transformation sees the bridal shop fly out of sight and streamers fall from above as 'The dance at the gym' begins. It starts with heavy blues that makes reference to ideas heard at the start of the prologue. The rhythm becomes fragmented as the Jets and Sharks withdraw to opposite sides of the dance floor. An adult tries to break the ice by getting the boys to form a circle around an inner circle of girls. The two circles promenade in opposite directions until a whistle blows – couples facing each other at this point are then expected to dance together. Bernstein writes this 'promenade' in an old-fashioned, ragtime-like style but with an occasional rasping dissonance in the bass to make it clear what the teenagers think of this kind of dancing.

The whistle blows, the music stops – and each Jet is left facing a Shark. The groups separate in disgust and begin a mambo, a Latin-American dance with driving rhythms from Cuba. The actual dancing begins with a rhythmic shout of 'Mambo! Mambo! Go!' and, as it turns into a challenge dance between the leading couples from each rival gang, the malevolent tritone makes its presence felt:

Towards the end of the mambo, Tony and Maria see each other for the first time. The lights dim, the dance floor clears, and they begin another popular Latin-American dance of the 1950s, the cha cha (it's name comes from the prominent use of a 'cha-cha-cha' rhythm at the ends of phrases). It is based on a transformation of the three-note figure shown by the lower brackets in example (f), which mutates into the dancing melody shown in (g), in which the tritone has immediately become less threatening by repeatedly resolving the dissonant

C♯ to a D. This melody is a stylised version of the show's hit song 'Maria' that is soon to appear:

The anticipation of 'Maria' becomes more obvious as this three-note motif becomes slower and more legato in the 'meeting scene' example (h) above. But before we hear the song itself the gangs return to a reprise of the Promenade. This is followed by 'Jump' – a dance from the swing era that looks forward to rhythm-and-blues with its strong backbeat and use of blue (i.e. flat) 3rds and 7ths. 'Jump' is played very quietly because, over the music, Bernardo pulls Maria from Tony's arms and plans with Riff a big showdown between their rival gangs.

Tony is left alone to sing 'Maria'. Sondheim's lyrics deserve special attention – he clearly realised that a love song about a girl Tony had met only five minutes ago would be implausible. And so the song is not about the girl herself, but the magic of her name. The accompaniment to the song is based on the rhythm of the habañera (another Cuban dance), seen in the bass of example (i), but the vocal part is much freer with circling triplets that echo Tony's whirling emotions:

This song also sees a beautiful transformation of the extended tritone motif. Adapted to fit the rhythm of Maria's name perfectly , it is rising and aspirational. The slow speed means that the tension of the chromatic A♮ is more obvious, but it finds immediate release by resolving to B♭. Bernstein leaves little doubt that Tony has found a resolution to conflict, both musical and dramatic, in Maria.

Bernstein's music reflects every nuance of the text. The circling triplets give way to decisive quavers for the realisation that 'suddenly that name will never be the same to me', and while the music for 'never be the same' echoes that of the previous bar, it is not *actually* the same. The third phrase rises higher as he thinks of kissing Maria, but it is the sound of her name that is inspirational, taking the following phrases ever upward.

Bernstein is not afraid of more obvious word-painting, such as the sudden **_pp_** at 'Say it soft' and the repetitions of Maria suggested by the phrase 'I'll never stop saying Maria' – but his melody for these repetitions also reflects the way that a star-struck lover might say 'Maria' over and over with different nuances. After a climax that requires a sustained top Bb from Tony, the habañera bass at last stops, its pervasive rhythm having served its purpose of demonstrating how totally Maria's Puerto-Rican world has infiltrated Tony's thoughts.

Finally and most magically, Bernstein reverses the last two notes of the 'Maria motif', making the rising interval a perfect 5th (Db–Ab) and turning the rising semitone into a falling one. Below this the accompaniment poignantly condenses the version of the motif seen in example (i) into a **_ppp_** cadential figure in which the tritone is heard harmonically:

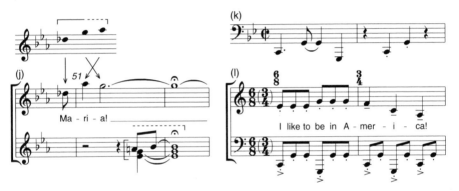

Next comes the 'balcony scene', with Tony and Maria's famous duet 'Tonight' in which, when the couple sing together, their notes are the same, except for being an octave apart, indicating that they are already of 'one heart' (to quote a later duet). Bernstein turns an old trick on its head in this number. To create an illusion of excitement, many composers of popular songs used to transpose successive verses up in semitones. Here Bernstein does the reverse. As the lovers become more intimate the key progressively drops in semitones. As the tempo gets slower and the pitch gets lower, much of the last part of the duet dissolves into a melodrama of spoken dialogue above music. At the end, the accompaniment looks forward to act two by quoting 'There's a place for us' – Bernstein's musical equivalent of Shakespeare's foreshadowing of destiny that is so central to *Romeo and Juliet*.

The next scene introduces a total change of mood, focusing on Anita and the Shark girls disputing the differences between Puerto Rico and the United States in the lively production number, 'America'. Bernstein demonstrates his grasp of Latin-American music (which he knew at first hand from visits to South America with his Chilean-born wife) in a range of techniques. In addition to Latin-American instruments such as the claves and guiro, the first section features one of the fundamental rhythms of Latin-American music – the bass ostinato pattern shown in example (k) above. The rhythm is known as the *3:2 son clave* because of the pattern of three notes in the first bar (in habañera rhythm) followed by two in the second. Over the top of this, Bernstein layers a complex texture of parts using crotchet- and minim-triplets.

For the main part of the number ('I like to be in America'), Bernstein uses a Mexican dance-style called the huapango. It is characterised by alternate bars of $\frac{3}{4}$ and $\frac{6}{8}$ at a fast tempo, as shown in example (l) above, with the $\frac{3}{4}$ bars providing the opportunity for a heavily emphasised 'America' at the end of every line in the choruses. 'America' fulfills an important function in the musical: it is the only musical number that the Sharks sing independent of the Jets and it offers light relief in a drama preoccupied with tension and despair ('Gee, Officer Krupke' serves a similar purpose in the second act). The sudden change in the audience's emotional response generated by these amusing interludes serves to intensify the high drama that follows.

The Jets are spoiling for a fight with the Sharks. In 'Cool', Riff issues a warning – 'You wanna live? You play it cool', spoken over the sinister bass pattern shown in example (m) that expresses the gang's pent-up energy:

The continued use of the tritone (C–F♯) is obvious. But example (m) also shows how tightly Bernstein's almost symphonic integration of *West Side Story* is developing. The rising perfect 4th followed by an augmented 4th (shown by the bracket above the stave) is none other than the three-note motif from the prologue that we heard when we first became aware of the tension between the rival gangs – compare it with examples (b) and (c) on page 53. Also, fatefully combined with this motif, is another augmented 4th variant – the 'Maria' motif, shown by the bracket under the stave.

Riff delivers his terse, clipped phrases to a melody based on example (m) – the opening of it is shown in example (n). After one verse a dance episode begins, for which Bernstein astonishingly writes a fugue, a texture more associated with church music than musicals. However, it is a jazz fugue, and its independent musical strands vividly portray the way each individual Jet lets off steam. The fugal texture gives way to *ff* octaves and drum breaks as the Jets come together to work out their frustrations in a ritualistic communal dance. After a yell, Riff's opening melody alternates with phrases from the fugue in a very loud and highly dissonant big-band style. Riff calms the gang down with a final verse – but only just, as the *ff* outbursts indicate. The number ends with finger-snaps, disintegrating fragments of the fugue, and an inversion of the opening 4ths motif. All is under control again. All is cool.

Tony meets Maria at the bridal shop, where they dream of marriage in the duet 'One hand, one heart'. In a complex quintet, Tony and Maria reprise their duet 'Tonight' while Anita, Riff and Bernardo simultaneously sing about the forthcoming fight ('The Jets are going to have their way tonight'). Maria has begged Tony to stop the conflict, but in the purely instrumental ending to Act 1 ('The rumble') Bernardo murders Riff and is then killed by Tony in revenge. Police sirens are heard and everyone runs. As the sinister 4ths motif reappears the curtain falls on a stage that is empty except for two dead bodies. In the entire history of the musical, audiences had never witnessed an Act 1 finale like it.

At the start of Act 2, Maria knows nothing of the tragedy the audience have just witnessed, making her delightful solo 'I feel pretty' all the more poignant. She is told the news that Tony has killed her brother; Tony then enters to explain how he acted in a moment of anger. She forgives him and they imagine running away to start a better life – an idea expressed in a symbolic ballet sequence ('Somewhere') in which singers voice the couple's dream that 'There's a place for us'. The dream turns into a nightmare, only returning to reality when the actual Tony and Maria, now in each other's arms, conclude the final phrases of the song.

As with 'America' in Act 1, such tense, high drama needs the relief of comedy before it can escalate further. In Act 2 this is provided by a 'comic policeman' sketch about the incompetent Officer Krupke who is trying to quiz the Jets on the murders at the end of Act 1. In 'Gee, Officer Krupke', Sondheim has a field day with the lyrics for their protestations, ranging from 'Our mothers all are junkies, our fathers all are drunks' to mention of every social taboo imaginable. Meanwhile, Bernstein starts this jolly number in B and ends it in F – the malevolent tritone permeates even the lightest moments of this musical drama.

Anita arrives and bitterly asks Maria how she could love 'A boy like that, who'd kill your brother'. Maria's response is the song 'I have a love', that touchingly includes a reference (example (o)) back to the melodic shape of 'Somewhere' (example (p)):

It convinces Anita that Maria loves Tony as much as she had loved Bernardo, and so Anita confides that Chino, one of the Sharks, has a gun and intends to murder Tony. Although Anita is a Shark, Maria persuades her to go to the Jets to warn Tony. But in the 'taunting scene' (which starts with the sound of a jukebox playing a pre-recorded version of the Act 1 mambo and ends with a distorted version of 'America') Anita is humiliated by the Jets and hysterically lies that Chino actually killed Maria, not Tony, in an act of revenge.

When Tony hears this, his dream of a future with Maria is shattered and he runs out into the street calling for Chino to kill him too. Suddenly a figure emerges from the shadows – it is Maria. As Tony rushes towards her, Chino appears and shoots him. The lovers manage only a few bars of 'Somewhere' before Tony dies in Maria's arms. There is no more singing. Maria takes the gun and wildly points it at the gang members who have gathered round – 'we all killed him' she cries, as she collapses in grief. The Jets and Sharks form pairs and process out with Tony's lifeless body, united at last through tragedy. As the curtain falls, circling fragments of 'Somewhere' (the aspirational song that the doomed lovers never get to complete in the work) resolve onto ethereal chords of C major. But deep in the orchestra, the tritone below C (F♯) still tolls its awesome warning. Only in the final bar of the work does it cease:

West Side Story remains one of the most original works in the history of the musical. It presents a plot rooted in violence and tragedy, exploring social tension, and making extensive use of contemporary dance in Jerome Robbins' very masculine choreography; it has a score that integrates ideas derived from opera, jazz and Latin-American music. Despite being a challenging work, it also contains a number of very popular songs and was a success on Broadway (although not to the same extent as *Oklahoma!* or *My Fair Lady*). Appreciation grew with the passage of time – the London production ran for three years until 1961, in which year *West Side Story* was adapted as a film musical, while amateur and professional stage productions have continued ever since.

The paradox of *West Side Story* is that, while it showed how a musical could be a vehicle for contemporary drama in a popular style that could raise serious issues, nobody was able to follow successfully in its footsteps. Even Bernstein's musical, *1600 Pennsylvania Avenue* (1976), with book and lyrics by the highly experienced Alan Jay Lerner, was one of Broadway's most famous flops, closing after only seven performances. Nevertheless, a number of successful, if more traditional, musicals appeared over the next few years including, in 1959, the final work from the team of Rodgers and Hammerstein, *The Sound of Music*.

One theme characterises these later works – unlike the contemporary setting of *West Side Story*, but echoing *My Fair Lady*, they invoke nostalgia for the past, almost all being set in the period from the 1890s to the 1940s.

Works from a new generation of composers included two huge successes in 1964. The first was *Hello, Dolly!*, which ran for 2,844 performances (exceeding the opening run of even *My Fair Lady*). The music and lyrics were by Jerry Herman (born 1931) and the book was by Michael Stewart, based on Thornton Wilder's play *The Matchmaker*. Set in the glamour of 1890s New York, it tells the story of a wily widow's pursuit of a wealthy new husband, and her success in pairing up a number of his staff and relations. Visually stunning, it includes the show-stopping production number (and title song) 'Hello, Dolly!'. Herman later wrote the score for *Mack and Mabel* (1974), which suffered from an unsympathetic production but is remembered for its fine music. The overture became world famous in 1982 as the music to which Torvill and Dean danced in the world figure-skating championships.

The other big hit of 1964 was *Fiddler on the Roof*, which became the longest-running Broadway musical to date, with an opening run of 3,242 performances. It was adapted to become an award-winning musical film in 1971. In contrast to the glitzy world of *Hello, Dolly!*, although set only a few years later in 1905, it tells a very human story of the struggle to maintain a traditional Jewish way of life in Tsarist Russia. The book by Joseph Stein is based on Sholom Aleichem's *Tevye* stories, the lyrics are by Sheldon Harnick and the music is by Jerry Bock. The memorable staging was the last major Broadway work by Jerome Robbins (the choreographer of *West Side Story*). The score includes a traditional waltz-song ('Matchmaker, matchmaker, make me a match') and an amusing take on the traditional romantic duet ('Do you love me?'), in which a couple who have been married for 25 years belatedly and reluctantly realise that they are actually in love. But the public particularly took to the songs in which Bock created a hint of traditional Jewish music, such as 'Sunrise, Sunset' in which a modal waltz tune is accompanied by minor-key harmonies, and the ever-famous 'If I were a rich man' with its constant shifts between major and parallel minor keys.

Kander and Ebb: *Cabaret*

Two years later, *Cabaret* (1966) proved to be one of the most original musicals of the decade. It combines a revue-like series of acts set in a seedy Berlin nightclub of the 1930s (effectively forming a 'show within a show') with dark undertones of the Nazi regime that was rising to power. The lyrics are by Fred Ebb and the music by John Kander, while the book by Joe Masteroff is based on John Van Druten's play *I am a Camera* (itself based on a collection of short stories by Christopher Isherwood). The team of Kander and Ebb were skilled in writing songs with a memorable period flavour that arise logically from the plot, carry the action forward and are able to stand alone, outside of the show, as hits in their own right.

Act 1 opens in the Kit Kat Klub, where the Master of Ceremonies (MC) and cabaret girls offer an international welcome:

A young American writer called Cliff has come to Berlin seeking inspiration for a new novel. He meets a German, Ernst, who suggests he stays at Fräulein Schneider's boarding house. After leaving his bags, Cliff goes to the Kit Kat Klub where he hears the British singer Sally Bowles perform 'Don't tell mama'. Each table in the club is connected by telephones, which patrons use to proposition one another, memorably illustrated in the 'Telephone dance': 'Table seven calling number three. How are you, handsome?' – 'You mean me?'. Sally chats to Cliff on the telephone, but declines his offer to see her home as it would make her boyfriend Max (the owner of the club) jealous. But next day Sally arrives at Fräulein Schneider's with the news that Max has thrown her out and asks to stay with Cliff in the song 'Perfectly marvelous'.

Back at the club, the liberal subculture of Berlin at that time is reflected in a highly suggestive trio in which the MC introduces his 'Two ladies'. The three of them 'switch partners daily to play as we please'. Meanwhile, at the boarding house, a romantic sub-plot develops between Fräulein Schneider and Herr Schultz, an elderly Jewish fruit-shop owner who presents her with the precious gift of a pineapple – 'It couldn't please me more' she sings in response. A shadow of things to come is heard in the next scene, in which the waiters at the club sing a chillingly nationalistic anthem, 'Tomorrow belongs to me'.

Some months have passed. Cliff is living in a dream ('Why should I wake up?') but Sally is pregnant and they need cash. When Ernst suddenly turns up, Cliff accepts his mysterious offer of money to deliver a suitcase to a client. At the club, the acts continue to reflect the drama outside as the MC explains that 'there's more than one way to make money' in the song 'Sitting pretty'; this breaks into a dance in which chorus girls represent currencies of different countries.

Herr Schultz proposes to Fräulein Schneider in the waltz-duet 'Married', and they celebrate their engagement with a party and dance at his fruit shop, at which Schultz sings about the Yiddish expression 'Meeskite'. But Ernst, now openly wearing a Nazi armband, warns Fräulein Schneider that marrying a Jew would be unwise. The first act ends with a reprise of 'Tomorrow belongs to me', which increasing numbers of the cast feel it politically prudent to join in with.

After an instrumental *entr'acte*, the MC and cabaret girls perform a kick-line dance, which scarily transforms into goose-step marching. Fräulein Schneider confesses her worries about marrying Schultz, who attempts to reassure her in a reprise of 'Married', which is suddenly interrupted by the ominous sound of a brick shattering his shop window. Back at the club, the MC again reflects what is happening in the outside world by means of a bizarre song and dance with a handbag-carrying gorilla ('If you could see her'). It ends with the spine-chilling message 'If you could see her through my eyes, she wouldn't look Jewish at all'.

Fräulein Schneider returns the engagement present from Cliff and Sally. The marriage is off, she has no other choice – 'What would you do?', she sings. Cliff wants to take Sally to America to raise their baby, but Sally still thinks Berlin is wonderful. He angrily tells her to wake up to what is going on around them. Sally storms back to the club for her show-stopping title song, 'What good is sitting alone in your room? Come hear the music play. Life is a cabaret, old chum, come to the cabaret'.

When Sally returns to her room, Cliff (who has been beaten up by two Nazis after refusing to run another errand for Ernst) notices that her fur coat is missing. Sally has sold it to pay for an abortion. Cliff leaves Berlin, broken-hearted. Sitting on the train, waiting for it to depart, Cliff reads aloud the start of his novel 'There was a city called Berlin, in a country called Germany. There was a cabaret, and there was a master of ceremonies. It was the end of the world, and I was dancing with Sally Bowles – and we were both fast asleep.' As he begins a reprise of the show's opening number, the train pulls away to reveal the MC and the Kit Kat Klub, who take over the singing. But it turns into a nightmarish sequence of musical reminiscences. German uniforms and swastikas dominate the now gloomy set. Sally is there: 'It'll all work out', she says, 'It's only politics, and what's that got to do with us?'. Finally the MC is left to finish the show alone in a distorted reflection of its opening, singing 'Auf Wiedersehen! A bientôt!' and, as the lights turn off, speaking an abrupt 'Goodnight'.

Substantial changes were made for the 1972 film version of *Cabaret*. Since it starred the American Liza Minelli, Sally Bowles was turned into a US citizen, while Cliff became an English character called Brian Roberts. The subplot was rewritten around two new characters and, to enhance the realism of the work, 'book songs' that advance the plot were cut. This restricts the music mainly to numbers performed inside the Kit Kat Klub, where they are accompanied (in new orchestrations) by an on-screen stage band. Kander and Ebb replaced 'Don't tell mama' with the much raunchier 'Mein Herr', while 'Sitting pretty' was replaced with a new song about money – the famous 'Money makes the world go round'.

Kander and Ebb continue to be remembered for their big show-stopping numbers, such as 'All that jazz' and 'Razzle dazzle', both from *Chicago* (1975) and the famous song 'New York, New York', written for the 1977 film of the same name. Ebb died in 2004, but their final collaboration, *Curtains* – a backstage musical murder mystery, premiered in summer 2006 to mixed reviews.

The musical in Britain

Almost all of the Broadway musicals mentioned earlier also had successful runs in London and other major cities in Britain. However, until the 1960s musicals by British composers had usually been lightweight comedies which, because they often played to a peculiarly English sense of humour, rarely crossed the Atlantic to New York. Noel Coward (1899–1973), famous for his stage plays, is also remembered as a composer of works that range from the operetta-like *Bitter Sweet* (1929) to revues such as *Words and Music* (1932), which features the song 'Mad dogs and Englishmen' and the ensemble 'Mad about the boy'. Coward's friend Ivor Novello (1893–1951) was a Welsh composer whose rather old-fashioned operetta-like musicals are characterised by romantic melodies, such as 'We'll gather lilacs in the spring again' from *Perchance to Dream* (1945).

Lionel Bart (1933–1999) began work in the theatre as an understudy and scene painter, also writing lyrics for several shows. In 1956 he became a member of Tommy Steele's skiffle group and started songwriting. His string of hits included *Livin' Doll* written in 1959 for Cliff Richard and in that same year he contributed lyrics and songs to two musicals that were based on life in London. Their success prompted Bart to start on his own big project, the musical *Oliver!* (1960). He wrote the book (based on Charles Dickens' novel *Oliver Twist*) as well as the lyrics and music. However, since Bart could hardly read music or play the piano, he sang his tunes into a tape recorder, and relied on others to harmonise and arrange them, particularly the experienced conductor and composer, Eric Rogers.

Oliver! was an outstanding success, with a strong cast and an innovative set built on a revolving stage. The musical numbers range from the nostalgic ballad, 'Where is love', through aspirational love-songs ('As long as he needs me'), sing-along waltz-songs ('Oom-pah-pah') and comedy songs ('Pick a pocket or two') to cheerful production numbers such as 'Food, glorious food' and 'Consider yourself one of us'. The work has a highly dramatic ending with an extended melodrama during which the villain Bill Sykes is shot while trying to abduct young Oliver Twist – although rather let down by the subsequent finale that reprises a medley of the show's jolliest tunes.

Oliver! was also successful on Broadway and was turned into a memorable musical film (without the stage-show finale) in 1968. Performances have continued ever since, the show being a particular favourite with schools and youth theatres. Time did not deal so kindly with Bart himself, whose subsequent musicals were increasingly unsuccessful. He bankrupted himself trying to rescue them, and later suffered from alcoholism and depression for many years.

In the 1950s, Lionel Bart had worked for Joan Littlewood's Theatre Workshop in Stratford, East London. It had developed a collective approach to drama in which the actors contributed to the creation of new works, one of which was *Oh, What a Lovely War* (1963). It is a compilation musical using songs that were popular during the First World War. The work satirises the war by contrasting optimistic music-hall songs and comic sketches with projected photographic images and statistics that reveal the true horror of the conflict. It was a surprise hit, transferring from Stratford to the West End and, in 1969, being turned into a film with a star-studded cast.

A collective approach produced another unexpected success in America a few years later. *A Chorus Line* (1975) began life as a series of tape-recorded interviews between director Michael Bennett and various experienced Broadway dancers. Bennett then asked Nicholas Dante and James Kirkwood to construct a book from their memories, while the songs were written by lyricist Edward Kleban and composer Marvin Hamlisch (who had arranged Scott Joplin's music for the film *The Sting* in 1973). The work continued to develop in workshop sessions before reaching its final form.

The result was a concept musical (see page 8 for a definition of this), not based around a plot like a book musical, but based on the concept of a Broadway chorus audition, in which the director requires the auditionees to share their memories and struggles, explain their love of dance and reveal their fears. The audience gradually learns more and more about each individual, only to see them all merge back into anonymity in the perfectly choreographed finale, 'One'. *A Chorus Line* ran for 15 years, its 6,137 performances holding the record for the longest Broadway run in history until 1997.

5

New directions

Until the 1960s, songs from successful new musicals would often feature in the pop charts. Even as late as 1964, Louis Armstrong's recording of the title song from *Hello, Dolly!*, made just before the show opened, pushed the Beatles off the number one spot in the US charts. However, by the end of the decade the increasing dominance of rock music left show tunes sounding old-fashioned, and musicals were losing the publicity offered by chart success. A new direction was needed.

The rock musical

Something altogether different appeared when *Hair* (1968) opened on Broadway. The slight plot, by librettists Gerome Ragni and James Rado, centres on the free-loving lifestyles of a group of hippies, their views on sex, poverty, race relations and war, and their rebellion against being drafted to fight in Vietnam. The show itself was a rebellion – the audience was invited on stage to dance, and the work contains nudity, obscene language and songs about drugs. *Hair* coincided with the abolition of theatrical censorship in the UK, being the first work to be publicly staged in London without a censor's licence since the beginning of the 17th century. The most memorable feature of *Hair* is its sheer number of songs (well over 30 in most versions of the show) written by Galt MacDermot. They include three lasting hits, 'Let the sunshine in', 'Good morning starshine' and, above all, 'Aquarius':

Godspell (1971) began life as a university project – a play by John-Michael Tebelak based on the account of Christ's adult life in the Gospel of Saint Matthew. In its original form, the songs used the words of various hymns, set to new tunes by members of the cast. The result was seen by two producers who spotted its Broadway potential and commissioned new music from Stephen Schwartz, who would later write for Disney and create the 2003 musical *Wicked*. *Godspell* was a huge success, remembered for songs such as 'Day by day', 'Turn back, O man' and 'Prepare ye the way of the Lord'. The last of these is typical of the songs in

Godspell. It starts with a simple unaccompanied phrase that is continually repeated as a riff while layer upon layer of parts are added to reach a stunning gospel-style climax:

Grease (1972) also began life as a modest play with incidental songs before its creators, Jim Jacobs and Warren Casey, were encouraged to develop it into a full-scale rock musical. Set in a high school in 1959, it centres on teenage life, romance and rebellion, and deals with issues such as pregnancy and gang violence. However, the musical style of *Grease* was not contemporary – most of the songs are in a pastiche of 1950s rock-and-roll idiom. Just as *Godspell* was far less controversial than the superficially similar *Jesus Christ Superstar* (see below), so *Grease* appealed to a much broader audience than *Hair*, and it became a long running hit in both New York and London. The 1978 film version of *Grease*, starring John Travolta and Olivia Newton-John, was equally successful, the movie's soundtrack becoming a number one album, and several of the individual numbers becoming chart-topping hits. *Grease* was revived on Broadway in 1994 and like *Godspell* has become a favourite musical for performance by community and school drama groups.

Another rock musical much enjoyed by such groups is *Little Shop of Horrors* (1982). The work began as an off-Broadway comedy, with music in 1960s pop styles by Alan Menken and a book by Howard Ashman. The latter is based on the black comedy film *The Little Shop of Horrors* (1960) about an inept florist who manages to raise a plant that feeds on human blood.

Andrew Lloyd Webber: *Jesus Christ Superstar*

In 1968, the composer Andrew Lloyd Webber and lyricist Tim Rice were commissioned to write a 15-minute concert work for the boys of Colet Court School in London. The result was *Joseph and the Amazing Technicolor Dreamcoat*, a contemporary and witty interpretation of the biblical story of Joseph. It was such a success that the school mounted a second performance in central London which attracted a favourable review in the national press. This led to an enlarged version of the work, which was published and recorded, thus launching Lloyd Webber's career as one of the best-known writers of modern musicals. *Joseph* was altered and enlarged several more times and by 1973 had become a successful full-length stage musical. There have been at least 12 different cast albums of the work and its 2007 revival was preceded by a national television competition to select a singer for the leading role. The work is much loved for its variety of styles, from traditional ballads such as 'Close every door to me' and 'Any dream will do' to witty pastiches of ragtime, calypso, French cabaret song, country music and even a parody of Elvis Presley in 'Song of the king' (marked '1957 Rock time' in the score and supplied with idiomatic 'Bop-shu-wah-doo-wah' responses).

Even before *Joseph* was staged, Rice and Lloyd Webber had already embarked on a far more ambitious project; *Jesus Christ Superstar* (1971), a full-length work based on Christ's last days on earth. It proved controversial because it focuses on Jesus as a human being (the resurrection is not included) who can become tired and irritated by his followers. It dwells on his personal struggle with Judas, surprisingly portrayed as a well-meaning if misguided individual. It also suggests that Mary Magdalene fell in love with Jesus, and it examines the role in which fame might have impacted on Christ's life (hence 'Superstar' in the title).

Jesus Christ Superstar was initially released in 1970 as a sound recording because producers were nervous of portraying such sensitive issues in the theatre. It was first staged (rather poorly) in New York in 1971 and (much more successfully) in London in 1972. It was clear that pre-releasing the music generated an enormous appetite for the show itself, and Lloyd Webber used this technique for some of his later works.

Because *Superstar* is through-composed, it is sometimes described as a 'rock opera'. It followed in the footsteps of the Who's *Tommy* (1969), a work that began life as a concept album but which was always intended for live, staged performance, and that is often regarded as the first 'rock opera'.

Superstar requires substantial vocal and instrumental resources, the latter including a large orchestra, piano, organ and Moog synthesiser, as well as lead guitar, rhythm guitar, bass guitar and drums. The work begins with a short overture that introduces some of the main musical motifs from the show, including:

Andrew Lloyd Webber

The first, heard on lead guitar at the very start of the overture, is a motif that becomes a symbol of unalterable destiny – it is the melody sung when the priests of the temple plot the downfall of Jesus ('This Jesus must die') and it is the melody sung by Pilate when Jesus is brought to trial ('And so the king is once again my guest'). The second is from the title song, which is not heard in full until near the end of the work.

Act one begins with Judas expressing doubts over Jesus's rising fame. The bass riff that accompanies his song 'Heaven on my mind' will return in Act 2, where it is heard (unaccompanied) 39 times, once for each of the 39 lashes of Christ that resulted from his betrayal by Judas.

The followers of Jesus have no such doubts, expressing their excitement about rumours of his triumphant journey to Jerusalem in the riff-based 'What's the buzz', with its reggae-like alternation of two chords (A^7 and D^7):

Seeing the irritation felt by Jesus as a result of such badgering, Mary Magdalene offers soothing ointment and reassurance in 'Everything's all right' – another riff-based song, but slower and in a quintuple metre, more associated with cool jazz than rock:

Jewish priests discuss what to do about the threat from Jesus and his growing number of followers ('This Jesus must die') but are interrupted by a production number built around the triumphal entry into Jerusalem that confirms Christ's 'superstar' status – the gloriously jubilant 'Hosanna, Hey-sanna, -sanna, -sanna, Ho-'. Jesus tells the high priest that putting an end to such hysteria is now impossible.

When Jesus goes to the temple in Jerusalem, he discovers that it has become a centre for money lending and vice of all kinds. Traders hawk their wares to the tune of the first breathless riff below (in another irregular metre):

After Jesus throws them out he is besieged by the lame and ill seeking to be cured. They are as out of control as the money lenders, and so Lloyd Webber uses the same urgent rhythm – but with the melody freely inverted so that the last word of 'Will you touch, will you mend me Christ?' ends with a desperate plea of 'Christ' on a top E. Mary Magdalene comforts the exhausted Jesus in a reprise of 'Everything's all right' and then, in a beautiful ballad, confesses that 'I don't know how to love him'. Act 1 ends with Judas accepting the high priest's offer of money in return for information on where Jesus can be arrested ('Blood money'). The last two bars before the interval are eerily recited by an off-stage children's choir singing 'Well done Judas … Good old Judas'.

Act 2 begins with 'The last supper'. Jesus, wracked with doubt about his mission, angrily turns on his followers and claims that nobody will remember him after he dies and that his closest friends will betray him. In 'Gethsemane' Jesus reluctantly accepts his destiny. The dull, plodding crotchets that expressed his weariness in the earlier temple scene are gloriously transformed into an aspirational melody as Christ accepts his godly father's 'cup of poison':

The rhythm is given life and the pitch is transposed up a 6th to produce a climax on 'cup' (the word used in the Biblical account: 'Father let this cup pass from me'). Pulsating inner parts increase the tension and the texture is thickened by sustained brass, organ, harp and the rock group. Above this edifice a glorious counter-melody on oboe and violins cascades in descending sequences full of heart-wrenching appoggiaturas. Lloyd Webber's ability to move easily from a rock-based idiom into such an overtly romantic style provides just the type of grand, operatic colour that has made many of his works so popular.

Jesus is betrayed by Judas, arrested and brought before King Herod. In *Superstar*, Lloyd Webber rarely employed the pastiche styles that give *Joseph* its variety, but he made an exception for King Herod, whose mocking insults are set in ragtime style, with tuba doubling the bass (as in early recordings of jazz) and a 'honky-tonk' piano part: 'So you are the Christ, you're the great Jesus Christ, prove to me that you're divine – change my water into wine'.

Judas, stricken with guilt over what he has done, expresses his remorse in a distorted reprise of 'I don't know how to love him', originally sung in Act 1 by Mary Magdalene, the repentant sinner. He hangs himself and the off-stage children are heard again, their words changed to 'So long Judas … Poor old Judas'. Jesus is brought before Pontius Pilate, who tries to counter the crowd's demands for a crucifixion by sentencing Jesus to 39 lashes, each accompanied by a repetition of the bass riff from Judas's opening song. The crowd still demands his death and Jesus is led away to the sound of the work's title song. The crucifixion is portrayed through a collage of dissonant, partly improvised, effects, above which Jesus speaks his last words. The work ends with Christ's body being laid in the tomb, accompanied by a purely instrumental movement in which the theme from 'Gethsemane' (quoted on page 69) is transformed into a serene adagio for horns and strings.

Jesus Christ Superstar has been staged many times around the world. A film adaptation, shot on location in Israel and elsewhere, was released in 1973, and another film version (which is closer to the stage show) appeared in 2000. Lloyd Webber followed up its success with a series of musicals famed for their staging, special effects and memorable tunes, although sometimes criticised for their lack of dramatic depth. Popular appeal, supported by heavy marketing, has become an increasingly important element in his work, seen in the adoption of a generally conservative musical style and a preference for set-piece numbers rather than for developing dramatic ideas through musical devices, such as motivic transformation. His later works include a further collaboration with Tim Rice, *Evita* (1978), containing the hit song 'Don't cry for me, Argentina'. Musicals to books and lyrics by other writers include the revue-like *Cats* (1981), famed for the song 'Memories', and *Starlight Express* (1984), remembered for its hydraulic ramps and roller-skating actors. Lloyd Webber's most famous work, *The Phantom of the Opera* (1986) is also his most lavish and operatic, and is still running in both London and New York, holding the record for the longest-ever Broadway run (a record previously held by *Cats*). A number of his later musicals have been less successful, particularly in America, and some have suffered from high production costs and poor reviews.

Stephen Sondheim: *Sweeney Todd*

In the 1970s, Stephen Sondheim (lyricist for *West Side Story*) established his reputation as a composer in a series of concept musicals, built around an issue (such as marriage or employment) that is illustrated by the plot. They include *Company* (1970) about a single man seeking love in New York, the melancholic *Follies* (1971) about theatrical illusion and the shaky marriages of two retired showgirls, and *A Little Night Music* (1973), which examines aspects of love in youth, maturity and old age, and includes the famous song 'Send in the clowns'.

Sondheim returned to the book musical for *Sweeney Todd, The Demon Barber of Fleet Street* (1979). Hugh Wheeler's script is based on both the 19th-century legend of the serial killer and the 1973 play *Sweeney Todd* by Christopher Bond. Sondheim wrote the lyrics as well as the score. The work explores Todd's role as an unjustly persecuted man who became a serial killer in his attempt to wreak revenge on the judge who raped his wife, stole his daughter and wrongly imprisoned him. In addition to the musical numbers, much of the dialogue is underscored by music. The work's dark subject matter and highly integrated score, in which music is used to further the drama, makes *Sweeney Todd* seem more like an opera than a musical. Indeed, productions have been given in opera houses as well as theatres.

A short (optional) prelude ends with the deafening sound of a factory whistle. On one level this is symbolic of the Victorian industrial age in which the work is set, but, on another more chilling level, it recurs throughout the work to signal moments when Todd slits another victim's throat with his razor. The singing begins with 'The ballad of Sweeney Todd', a chorus which recurs many times and frames the work by returning at the end. The words invite the audience to 'Attend the tale of Sweeney Todd', while the modal melody and long-held drones in the accompaniment create the mood of a timeless folk-legend. The climax of the song ('Swing your razor wide, Sweeney') is ominously based on the traditional chant for the Dies irae ('Day of wrath') from the requiem mass. Sondheim disliked the artificial way in which the members of a chorus in a traditional musical all sing together, so this opening number includes vocal polyphony, in which several different melodies (each with their own words) overlap, just as a crowd might shout out different things simultaneously.

Sondheim uses numerous motifs that he transforms for dramatic purpose. For example, the sailor who returns to London with Todd expresses his delight at being back in the city with a three-note motif that returns to reflect his joy on meeting Todd's daughter, Johanna – later it is distorted by the judge, who is lusting after the same girl:

I have sailed the world,   Jo-han-na,   Jo-han-na,

Sondheim also uses motifs for dramatic foreshadowing. For instance, when a beggar woman near the start of the work lewdly propositions Todd, the melody she sings is transformed into a minuet in a dream sequence in which the judge rapes Todd's wife. The significance of this only becomes apparent much later – the woman's cry of 'Alms, alms' was sung to a falling semitone (the same descending interval heard whenever she appears). When Todd recalls the wife he thinks is dead ('My Lucy lies in ashes') he sings her name to the same falling semitone. And when Todd realises, after murdering the beggar woman, that she is the wife he hasn't seen for 15 years, the moment of recognition is marked by that same falling semitone, to which, in horror, he sings 'Lucy'.

Such musical, dramatic irony permeates the work. The bodies of Todd's victims are disposed of by Mrs Lovett, who turns them into meat pies. Her simple assistant, Tobias, has an inkling of what Sweeney Todd has been doing, and reassures Mrs Lovett that he will protect her: 'Nothing will harm you'. When Todd and Lovett realise that Tobias knows too much, they desperately try to get him to come out of hiding, transforming the motif to 'Nothing's gonna harm you' – which, of course, is quite the opposite of their murderous intent.

Although much of the musical idiom is strikingly modern, Sondheim drew on older styles to help portray the Victorian setting, including ballads, music hall and parlour songs. There is even a parody of Italian opera for the scene in which Signor Pirelli enters into a hair-cutting competition with Sweeney Todd – although, having lost, he goes the same way as Todd's other victims.

Sondheim's uses of the old device of a waltz-song are particularly effective. Act 1 ends with a duet in waltz style, in which Todd expounds Brechtian philosophy: 'The history of the world, my sweet … is who gets eaten and who gets to eat' as he and Mrs Lovett plan such recipes as 'shepherd's pie peppered with actual shepherds on top'. In its counterpart in Act 2, Todd reprises the same phrase to the words 'The history of the world, my pet … is learn forgiveness and try to forget' as he waltzes Mrs Lovett straight into a red-hot oven in his final murder of the show.

Despite such moments, much of the score is challenging, particularly in the highly dissonant 'Epiphany' that occurs just before the end of the first act, in which Todd (having just missed the chance to murder the judge) asserts, over recollections of many earlier motifs, that his mission is vengeance and that 'we all deserve to die'.

Critics, while recognising that Sweeney Todd is probably Sondheim's finest work, have often speculated about whether it should be regarded as an opera rather than a musical (Sondheim himself described it as a 'musical thriller'), but the producer George Martin has pointed to two indications that the work is essentially a musical. One is the nature of the finales to the two acts. The logical culmination of Act 1 is 'Epiphany', but its fragmentary phrases do not create a satisfactory ending and so Sondheim tacks on the amusing, but ultimately inconsequential, duet about meat pies. Similarly, in Act 2, the finale adds nothing new, as it normally would in opera – it is merely the 'framing' reprise of 'The ballad of Sweeney Todd'.

The other is Sondheim's attitude to orchestration. While most opera composers create their own individual sound worlds by notating every detail of the orchestral colour they require, Sondheim (like many composers of musicals) handed this vital task to Jonathan Tunick, a professional orchestrator. However, Sondheim's *laissez-faire* attitude to orchestration has produced a surprising consequence. One of the most successful recent revivals of Sweeney Todd has been a production in which the actors themselves play their own accompaniment on stage in a scaled-down instrumentation. First heard at the Watermill Theatre in Newbury, this innovative production toured in England before transferring to the West End and it subsequently formed the basis of the 2005 Broadway revival of the work. A film version of *Sweeney Todd*, starring Johnny Depp as Todd, was released in December 2007.

Sondheim's work, with its subtle use of music to delineate character and motivation, stands in marked contrast to public taste in the 1980s for such 'mega-musicals' as *Evita*, *The Phantom of the Opera* and, indeed, *Les Misérables*.

Claude-Michel Schönberg: *Les Misérables*

Claude-Michel Schönberg (born 1944) is a French singer, record producer and song-writer. He and librettist Alain Boublil wrote France's first rock opera in 1973, but the pair were little known to the rest of the world until their epic musical *Les Misérables* (Paris, 1980) was rewritten and translated into English for enormously successful runs in London (starting 1985 and still being performed in 2008) and on Broadway (1987–2003) where it had the third-longest run in history, after *The Phantom of the Opera* and *Cats*.

Les Misérables is largely through-composed, with little spoken dialogue, and is based on Victor Hugo's 1862 novel of the same title. It centres on the life of Jean Valjean, released on parole from prison in 1815 after serving 19 years for stealing bread to feed his family. Pitted against Valjean is the policeman Javert, who dedicates his life to an obsessive pursuit of Valjean for breaking parole.

Valjean finds that the yellow parole ticket (which, by law, he must wear) marks him out as an outcast to all except a kindly bishop who offers help. Valjean, embittered by his unjust imprisonment, steals from the bishop and is caught by the police. He is astonished when the bishop deliberately misleads the authorities to get Valjean off the hook and presents Valjean with a precious gift to help him start a new life.

Eight years later and Valjean has changed his name and used the bishop's gift to start a career which has led him to become a successful factory owner and mayor of a small town. Fantine, one of his workers, is thrown out of her job because she has an illegitimate child, and tells her story in one of the show's most famous songs:

Desperate for money to buy medicines for her sick daughter, Fantine becomes a prostitute but is arrested. Valjean, as mayor, ensures that she is taken to hospital rather than prison. Javert appears and announces that 'Valjean' has been re-captured but the mayor, knowing that it must be the wrong man, confesses that he is the real Valjean. Before returning to prison he visits the dying Fantine and promises that he will find and look after her daughter, Cosette, but Javert refuses to give Valjean any more time – in the ensuing fight, Valjean knocks the policeman out and goes on the run.

Meanwhile, Fantine's daughter has been taken in by the villainous Thénardiers, who run an inn, treating Cosette like Cinderella while indulging their own daughter, Eponine. Valjean finds Cosette and pays the Thénardiers to release the girl so that he can take her to a better life in Paris.

Nine years pass and Paris is on the brink of revolution. Among the gangs that roam the streets is one, led by Thénardier, that sets upon Valjean and Cosette. In a bitter twist of fate, they are rescued by Javert, who does not recognise Valjean until after he has got away. Meanwhile, a student named Marius tries to find Cosette, whom he loves, and persuades Thénardier's daughter Eponine to help him. She leads him to Valjean's house and waits outside while Marius expresses his love for Cosette. But Eponine spots her father and his gang surrounding the house intending to rob Valjean. She screams a warning and Cosette tells Valjean that she saw shadows. Convinced that it was Javert, he says they must prepare to leave France. Marius thinks he will never see Cosette again and returns to his student friends to prepare for the revolution.

Act 2 begins with the students building a barricade. Marius gives Eponine a letter to take to Cosette, which is intercepted by Valjean who consequently learns of their love. Eponine herself is secretly in love with Marius, and sings of her dreams of a love that will never be returned:

Back at the barricade, Eponine is shot in the fighting, and dies in Marius's arms. Meanwhile, Javert has been exposed to the students as a government spy. Valjean, who has gone to the barricade to look for Marius, is given the chance to execute Javert, but instead lets him go saying that he doesn't blame Javert for doing his duty.

In a fearsome battle the next morning, everyone at the barricade dies except for Valjean, who manages to escape into the sewers of Paris, carrying the wounded and unconscious Marius on his back. Thénardier is there, stripping the dead of their valuables and, while Valjean's back is turned, he takes a ring from Marius' finger. Valjean manages to get Marius out into the light, but Javert is waiting for them. Valjean asks to be allowed to take Marius to a doctor, after which he will return and surrender. As Javert waits he reflects on the goodness of Valjean. Overcome with guilt at his own relentless pursuit of a man so clearly reformed, Javert jumps to his death in the swollen River Seine.

Marius recovers in Cosette's care. Since they plan to marry, Valjean tells Marius of his past, but makes him promise not to tell Cosette and insists that after the marriage he must go away to avoid putting them in danger. On the wedding day Thénardier arrives to denounce Valjean as a murderer – Thénardier saw him carrying a body through the sewers and for proof shows Marius the ring he took from the 'corpse'. Marius sees that it is his own ring and thus realises, for the first time, that it was Valjean who saved his life that night.

In the final scene, Valjean is dying – without Cosette he has nothing more to live for. The wedded couple arrive in time for Marius to thank Valjean for saving his life, and for Cosette to learn the truth about her mother, before the old man dies and joins the spirits of Fantine, Eponine and the students who died manning the barricades.

This long story (the full musical runs for well over three hours), with its complex plot and contrived tear-jerking ending, seems more like a 'soap opera' than one of the most successful musicals in history. But perhaps that is one of the reasons for its success. The public loved its epic quality, encompassing the weaknesses and strengths of a flawed but ultimately redeemed ordinary man over a long period of time, involving the myriad of people who affected his life, personal and political struggles, and a love story – all played out against the dramatic background of revolutionary France. Added to this are the succession of uncomplicated, mainly strophic songs by Schönberg, and a colourful and engaging production aided by hydraulically-operated platforms and revolving stages. All of this helped place *Les Misérables* alongside *The Phantom of the Opera* (launched in London the following year) as one of the most successful 'mega-musicals' of its era.

Schönberg and Boublil had another great hit with *Miss Saigon* (1989), a modern re-telling of the plot of Puccini's emotive opera *Madame Butterfly* about a far-eastern woman destroyed by a doomed romance with an American marine. Their later collaboration, *Martin Guerre* (1996), loosely based on a real story from medieval France, proved less successful, despite numerous rewrites.

Elton John: *The Lion King*

The original version of *The Lion King* (1994) was a Disney animated feature film that made significant use of computer-manipulated graphics. It tells the story of a young African lion called Simba, born to be the king of all lions. His uncle, who would have been next in line to the throne, kills Simba's father and tricks Simba into blaming himself. Simba runs away, leaving his uncle to assume the role of king. Some years later, Simba is older and wiser, and returns for a final battle with his uncle. He wins the battle and takes up his rightful position as king, thus completing the 'circle of life'. The basis of this story – a young prince who plots revenge on his uncle for killing his father and usurping the throne – is the same timeless legend on which Shakespeare based his play *Hamlet*, although Disney's film has a far happier outcome than the Shakespearean tragedy.

Musicals

The British songwriter Elton John was commissioned to compose five songs for the film, to lyrics by Tim Rice. Elton John himself sang one of the most famous songs, 'Can you feel the love tonight', heard during the final credits:

In addition to the five songs, *The Lion King* has a score, written by the experienced film composer, Hans Zimmer, supplemented with material from the South-African singer Lebo Morake. Lebo M, as he is known, sings 'Nants ingonyama' (Swahili for 'There comes a lion') during the opening title sequence.

One of the most famous songs in the film is 'The lion sleeps tonight':

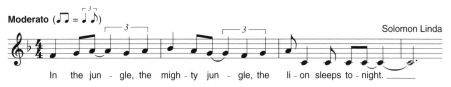

It is a song that has a fascinating history. It was composed and recorded by the South-African Zulu musician Solomon Linda in 1939 under the title 'Mbube' (Zulu for 'lion') and became enormously popular in South Africa. More than a decade later, the original recording was discovered by musicologist Alan Lomax and passed to his friend Pete Seeger, who recorded it in 1952 with his folk group the Weavers under the title 'Wimoweh'. It became a folk-music 'classic' and was covered by other bands, including the pop group the Tokens, for whom it was rewritten and retitled 'The lion sleeps tonight', achieving a US number one hit in 1961.

Many covers of all three versions were subsequently made, but original singer Solomon Linda had died in poverty in 1962, having sold the rights to the song for what amounts to little more than small change. However, under the law of the time, those rights should have reverted to Linda's descendants in 1987. Following the end of apartheid in South Africa, Solomon Linda's plight became a celebrated example of the West's exploitation of native African talent – one journalist estimated that the income from just the song's use in the *The Lion King* (a highly profitable film) was worth millions of pounds. Following a television documentary on the subject, and with support from the South-African government, the descendants of Solomon Linda brought a successful lawsuit against Disney which, in 2006, resulted in a substantial payment being made to a trust that will support South-African musicians.

The film of *The Lion King* was adapted as a stage musical with the same title in 1997, in which form it has become as popular as the original animated film, with productions in London, Broadway and national tours still running ten years later, as well as runs in Germany, France, Japan, South Korea and South Africa. Several changes and additions were made for the stage show, including new material from Lebo M and Hans Zimmer, and three new songs from Tim Rice and Elton John – a patter song called 'The morning report' (which was added to the video re-release), a witty vaudeville number entitled 'The madness of King Scar' and the rock-and-roll style 'Chow down'.

The original animation was reinterpreted with actors in elaborate animal costumes, some of whom were on stilts, with the addition of some life-size puppets. The production makes extensive use of special effects, including a complex aerial ballet with dancers on wires, and hydraulic motors to raise and lower various areas of the stage, placing it very much in the 'mega-musical' tradition that arose in the last two decades of the 20th century.

Elton John later wrote the music for *Billy Elliot: The Musical* (2005), The show has a book and lyrics by Lee Hall, who wrote the screenplay for the film *Billy Elliot* (2000) on which the musical is based. It tells the moving story of a boy who overcomes the prejudices of his working-class background to fulfil a dream of becoming a ballet dancer. The original film used a compilation of hits from the 1970s and 1980s by groups such as T. Rex, The Clash and The Jam. Elton John, who conceived the idea of turning it into a stage show, wrote an entirely new score that ranges in style from folk and rock to show tunes and anthems. It integrates with the plot and avoids the imposition of obvious 'breakout' numbers designed primarily to become hits outside the show.

Billy Elliot: The Musical won numerous awards for the best musical of 2005 and it looks set for a long run in London. It opened in Australia in December 2007 and will open on Broadway in September 2008.

Compilation musicals

Compilation musicals, based on a collection of pre-existing songs, are nothing new. The musical film *Singin' in the Rain* (1952) was an early example, and it could even be said that *The Beggar's Opera* was a type of compilation since it drew on a variety of well-known songs, supplied with new words. In both cases the songs contributed to a well-written, plausible plot.

In recent years, a new type of compilation musical has become popular, in which a slender plot is devised to link cover versions of songs by a well-known singer or group. One of the earliest was *Buddy – The Buddy Holly Story* (1989), but the genre did not really start to flourish until the turn of the century, with *Saturday Night Fever* (1999, using the music of the Bee Gees), *Mamma Mia!* (1999, based on the songs of Abba) and *We Will Rock You* (2002, using songs by Queen). There is little sign of enthusiasm for 'jukebox' musicals abating since they have become an important marketing tool to help keep older pop music in the public eye. The year 2006 alone saw the premieres of *Ring of Fire* (music of Johnny Cash), *Hot Feet* (Earth, Wind and Fire), *Dusty: The Original Pop Diva*

(Dusty Springfield), *Daddy Cool* (Boney M) and *The Times They Are A-Changing* (Bob Dylan), while 2007 saw the filming of *Mamma Mia!* ready for release in 2008.

These 'jukebox' or 'tribute' musicals are often little more than colourfully staged concerts. For example, *We Will Rock You* is set in the future at a time when all music is automatically generated by computers. Composers and musical instruments are banned and rock music is unknown. A group of rebels discover a video of Queen and go about recreating some of the group's greatest hits. The precise songs tend to vary according to the target audience of the particular production, but the show generally ends with a rousing performance of 'Bohemian rhapsody'. 'Jukebox' musicals appeal to impresarios because they require little expenditure on new material and, since the songs are already popular, good audiences are assured at minimal financial risk.

The compilation principle has also extended to musical films, although in a slightly different way. *Moulin Rouge!* (2001) drew on more than 40 years' worth of popular music, from the title song of *The Sound of Music*, through music by David Bowie, the Police, Queen, Elton John, Madonna and Nirvana to the song 'Chamma Chamma' from the Hindi film *China Gate*.

Similarly, the animated feature film about penguins, *Happy Feet* (2006), draws on songs made famous by Frank Sinatra, Elvis Presley, the Beach Boys, The Beatles, Stevie Wonder, Lionel Richie, Prince, and Queen, among others, linked by the device that every penguin must have its own unique song in order to attract a mate, and that some penguins need music for dancing.

Musical futures

According to statistics gathered by the American League of Theatres and Producers, 12.31 million tickets for Broadway shows were sold in the 2006–7 season, compared with 6.53 million in that of 1985–6. The Society of London Theatres reported that 2006 was the best season on record, with 12.36 million ticket sales compared to 10.24 million in 1986. In both cases it is estimated that musicals account for over 60% of the total ticket sales figures for theatres.

It may therefore seem strange that at a time when the musical has rarely been more popular, critics are questioning its future. The reason can be seen in the nature of the shows running on Broadway and in the West End. The majority are either 'mega-musicals', such as *The Phantom of the Opera*, which have been running for years and that rely heavily on stage effects for their popularity, or revivals from the past with a certified track record, such as *The Sound of Music*, or 'jukebox' musicals like *Mamma Mia!*, that offer a well-staged concert rather than a dramatic theatrical experience.

Truly original voices, like that of Stephen Sondheim, are very much in the minority. Sondheim summed up his own view in an interview for the *New York Times Magazine* in 2000, where he described the public's love of musicals as 'seeing what is familiar' – a by-product of the 'recycled culture' of modern life. The same concern was echoed in Britain in a 2003 submission to the House of Commons Select Committee on Culture, Media and Sport:

> 'The commercial nature of most of London's theatres has encouraged long-running blockbusters and revivals and, more recently, shows based on the well-known back catalogues of pop and rock stars. These trends however are driven by commercial considerations and have done a disservice to new writers and composers who have found it difficult to find theatre space to showcase their work or to persuade producers and theatre managers to take the risks involved in presenting new or unfamiliar musicals.'

It is certainly true that the public's demand for lavish spectacle has driven up costs to such an extent that few impresarios will risk promoting innovative or experimental new musicals. Indeed, even as established a figure as Andrew Lloyd Webber is no guarantee of financial success for a production– despite long runs, the weekly operating costs and other expenses of his *Sunset Boulevard* (1993) were so high that it is estimated to have lost at least 20 million dollars in the United States.

However, the musical has survived many previous crises of doubt about its future and the genre often re-emerges in some invigorating new way, as happened with the first book musicals and the first rock operas. In recent years, new influences from India have started to make their impact on the West. The enormous success of the Bollywood film industry has now spread to many other parts of the world, and is enjoyed by native as well as immigrant audiences. The International Indian Film Academy Awards have been held in London (2000) and Yorkshire (2007) to great acclaim. Bollywood films maintain many aspects of the traditional musical; catchy music (which is becoming increasingly westernised), elaborately choreographed song-and-dance numbers, brilliant costumes, vivid settings, comedy, thrills and simple plots about love triangles, angry parents, family disputes, long-lost relatives and unexpected reversals of fortune.

The influence of Bollywood on the stage musical was first seen in *Bombay Dreams* (2002). The music was written by the Indian film composer A. R. Rhaman, the lyrics by Don Black (who wrote the book and lyrics for several of Andrew Lloyd Webber's later musicals), and the work was produced by Lloyd Webber. It ran for two years in London, but was less successful in New York.

Rahman's work is being heard again in *Lord of the Rings* (2007), based on the epic novel by J. R. R. Tolkien. Completely rewritten after the musical's earlier unsuccessful run in Toronto, and laden with special effects, including a stage operated by 17 hydraulic motors, it is one of the most expensive shows ever to be mounted and suggests that the age of the 'mega-musical' has not yet passed. However, music plays a smaller role in the work than in most musicals – its creators have stated that they aimed for a dramatisation of the work that merely uses some of the conventions of a musical. Also, it follows in the path of *The Lion King* by drawing together composers from different musical traditions to contribute to the score. Some songs are written by the Finnish new age folk group Värttinä (Tolkien was influenced by the Finnish epic poem, *Kalevala*) and others are written by A. R. Rhaman – each sometimes reinterpret the other's work – and the whole is coordinated by the orchestrator, Christopher Nightingale.

This is a considerable departure from the traditional musical, in which one composer is responsible for the entire work, even if orchestrations and arrangements are handled by someone different. Will it point to a new direction in the history of the musical? The public are fickle, and only time will tell, but musicals have been adept at reinventing themselves over the years. As Oscar Hammerstein II once observed:

> 'It is nonsense to say what a musical should or should not be. It should be anything it wants to be, and if you don't like it you don't have to go to it. There is only one absolutely indispensable element that a musical must have. It must have music. And there is only one thing that it has to be – it has to be good.'
>
> Quoted by Stanley Green in *The World of Musical Comedy*
> (Ziff Davis Publishing, 1960), page 7

6
Chronology and resources

It is not unusual for changes to be made to a musical after, or even during, its initial run as well as for later revivals. In addition, substantial alterations are generally made if a stage musical is subsequently filmed. Such changes may include adding new songs, rewriting dialogue and removing unwanted material. Therefore there is often no definitive version of many musicals, and it should be expected that the scores and recordings in this selective list of musicals may not exactly match each other or precisely concur with any particular production seen on stage.

Vocal scores of musicals are often very expensive but may be available on loan from public libraries and can often be purchased second-hand. As an alternative, selections of the more famous songs from almost all of these musicals are available for considerably less than the price of a complete vocal score. Scripts of some musicals have been published, but in other cases are only available on hire as part of a set of performance material. The information below includes details of recommended recordings, but in many cases alternatives are available.

1925 *No, No, Nanette*

Music by Vincent Youmans, book by Otto Harbach and Frank Mandel, lyrics by Irving Caesar and Otto Harbach, based on Mandel's 1919 play, *My Lady Friends*. The vocal score is out of print, but selected songs (notably 'I want to be happy' and 'Tea for two') are published in various collections of songs from the period. The original cast recording of the 1971 Broadway version is available on CD (CBS/Sony SMK60890).

1927 *Show Boat*

Music by Jerome Kern, book and lyrics by Oscar Hammerstein II based on the 1926 novel of the same name by Edna Ferber. Vocal score published by Hal Leonard / Music Sales. A DVD of the 1951 film version is available on Warner Home Video. The 1987 three-CD audio recording on EMI 3615432 restores many items that had been cut from the original show.

1934 *Anything Goes*

Music and lyrics by Cole Porter. Original book by Guy Bolton and P. G. Wodehouse, substantially rewritten by Howard Lindsay and Russell Crouse. The vocal score published by Chappell is now out of print, but a vocal selection (based on the 1987 Broadway revival) is available from Warner Brothers. The 1956 film version is available on DVD from Paramount, but it is a poor adaptation that bears little relation to the original musical. The 2003 recording of the National Theatre's production is available on CD from First Night (CASTCD90). A CD of the 1989 studio recording with the London Symphony Orchestra is available on EMI/Angel (7-49848-2).

1935 *Porgy and Bess*

Music and lyrics by George Gershwin, DuBose and Dorothy Heyward, and Ira Gershwin. Based on the 1925 novel *Porgy* by DuBose Heyward, and its 1927 adaptation as a stage play by DuBose and Dorothy Heyward. Vocal score published by IMP / Alfred Publishing. Script: see page 86. A recording of the Glyndebourne Opera production is available from EMI on DVD (DVB4924969) and CD (4768362).

1943 *Oklahoma!*

Music by Richard Rodgers, book and lyrics by Oscar Hammerstein II based on the 1931 play *Green Grow the Lilacs* by Lynn Riggs. Vocal score published by Williamson Music. A DVD of Trevor Nunn's acclaimed 1998 production for the Royal National Theatre is available from Image Entertainment (ID1057 OKDVD) and musical numbers from the same production are available on CD from First Night Records (CASTCD69). The 1955 film version of *Oklahoma!* is available on DVD from 20th Century Fox Home Entertainment (0702001001).

1948 *Kiss Me, Kate*

Music and lyrics by Cole Porter, book by Samuel and Bella Spewack, loosely based on Shakespeare's play *The Taming of the Shrew* of c.1593. Vocal score published by IMP. Script: see page 86. A DVD of the Victoria Palace Theatre production, filmed live in 2002, is available from TDK (DVMCKMK). A CD of the 1987 production by the Royal Shakespeare Company is available from First Night Records (OCRCD6020).

1952 *Singin' in the Rain*

A musical film based on pre-existing songs. A song album of 11 numbers from the musical is published by IMP. The original film is available on DVD from Warner Home Video (D065621). In 2006, Warner brought out a special edition version on two DVDs (D065621), which also includes an out-take, documentary features and extracts from many of the films for which the songs were originally written. A special edition CD of the soundtrack and other items is also available from Warner (81227-4497-2).

1956 *My Fair Lady*

Music by Frederick Loewe, book and lyrics by Alan Jay Lerner based on George Bernard Shaw's 1913 play, *Pygmalion*. Vocal score published by Chappell, libretto published by Penguin. The 1964 film version is available on a single DVD from Warner Home Video (D016668S) – their alternative two-disc DVD provides additional material of only peripheral interest. Of the many CDs available, the cast recording of the National Theatre's 2001 revival presents a more stage-like interpretation of the work than the film version and is available on First Night (CASTCD83).

1957 *West Side Story*

Music by Leonard Bernstein, book by Arthur Laurents, lyrics by Stephen Sondheim, loosely based on Shakespeare's play *Romeo and Juliet* of c.1595. Vocal score and full study score published by Boosey and Hawkes (both including controversial revisions made by Bernstein shortly before his death). Script: see page 86. The 1961 film version of the show is available from MGM on a single DVD (15930DVD) or (with additional material) as a two-disc special edition (15930CDVD) or collector's edition (15930BCDVD). Songs from the film soundtrack are available on a budget-price CD from Sony (SK 48211). Bernstein's 1984 studio recording for the BBC is musically superior (with opera singers taking the main roles), and is available from Deutsche Grammophon on both DVD (0730179) and CD (457-199-2).

1960 *Oliver!*

Music and lyrics by Lionel Bart, based on the 1838 novel *Oliver Twist* by Charles Dickens. Vocal score published by Lakeview/Music Sales. A CD of the original London cast recording from 1960 is available on Decca Soundtrack (820590). A CD of the 1994 revival is available on First Night (CASTCD93). A DVD of the film version of *Oliver!* is available from Sony Pictures Home Entertainment (CDR10048).

1966 *Cabaret*

Music by John Kander, lyrics by Fred Ebb, book by Joe Masteroff based on John Van Druten's 1951 play *I am a Camera* (which was itself based on Christopher Isherwood's novel *Goodbye to Berlin*, published in 1946). Vocal score published by Time Square Publishing/Music Sales. Script: see page 86. A DVD of the 1972 film version is available from Prism Leisure/ Fremantle Home Entertainment (FHED1833), who also produce a widescreen version (FHED1444). A CD of a re-mastered version of the original film soundtrack is available from Sony/Columbia Legacy (SK60533).

Musicals

1971 *Jesus Christ Superstar*

Music by Andrew Lloyd Webber, lyrics by Tim Rice. A selection of nine songs from the show is published by MCA Music. Script: see page 86. A DVD of the 1973 film version is available from Universal Pictures (8232975) who also produce a DVD (0780712) of the 2000 film version, which is closer to the original stage show. Of the many available CDs of the work, the original recording made before it was staged is often considered the best, and is available on CD from MCA/Decca (0006634).

1979 *Sweeney Todd, the Demon Barber of Fleet Street*

Music and lyrics by Stephen Sondheim, book by Hugh Wheeler, based on the legend of Sweeney Todd and a 1973 play by Christopher Bond. A vocal score is published by Warner/Alfred Music Publishing. The 1982 television recording of the work is available on DVD from Warner Home Video (6750). The soundtrack of this recording is available on a double CD from RCA (3379-2-RC). A cast recording of the 2005 Broadway revival, in which the actors also form the band, is available on CD from Nonsuch (60533). A film version of the work, starring Johnny Depp as Todd and Helena Bonham-Carter as Mrs Lovett, was released in December 2007.

1980 *Les Misérables*

Music by Claude-Michel Schönberg, libretto by Alain Boublil, based on the 1862 French novel of the same name by Victor Hugo. A selection of songs from the show is published by Hal Leonard/Music Sales. The DVD produced by 2 Entertain Video (VCD0435) is of a concert version, not the stage show. A double CD of the original London cast recording is available on First Night (ENCORECD1).

1997 *The Lion King*

Songs by Elton John (to lyrics by Tim Rice), Solomon Linda and others, score by Hans Zimmer. Overlapping selections of songs from the film and later stage show version are published by Hal Leonard/Disney. A special edition DVD of the film is available from Disney on DVD (BED888911) who also produce the soundtrack on CD (3532212). An original cast CD of the Broadway show is available on Disney 3532162.

2005 *Billy Elliot: The Musical*

Music by Elton John, book and lyrics by Lee Hall, adapted from the film *Billy Elliot* (2000) written by Lee Hall. An album of 15 songs is available from Wise Publications/Music Sales. A CD of the original cast recording is available on Polydor (9875216). The original film of Billy Elliot is available on DVD, but this contains entirely different music from the stage show version. At the time of writing, brief video clips from the stage show were available for free viewing at: www.billyelliotthemusical.com.

2007 *Lord of the Rings*

Music by Finnish folk music band Värttinä and A. R. Rhaman, orchestrated by Christopher Nightingale. Book and lyrics Shaun McKenna and Matthew Warchus, based on J. R. R. Tolkien's epic fantasy novel of the same title, completed in 1949. An original cast CD of the London production is available from Kevin Wallace Music (EAN5051565100129). At the time of writing, brief video clips from the stage show were available for free viewing at www.lotr.com.

Further reading

Many books on musicals focus primarily on matters such as dates and photographs of productions, cast lists, length of runs, and so forth. In contrast, the following volumes include some detailed analyses and/or good overall coverage of the subject:

Block, G. *Enchanted Evenings: The Broadway Musical from Show Boat to Sondheim.* Oxford University Press, 2003.

Everett, W. A. and Laird, P. R. (eds.) *The Cambridge Companion to the Musical.* Cambridge University Press, 2008.

Grant, M. N. *The Rise and Fall of the Broadway Musical.* Northeastern University Press, 2005.

Riddle, P. H. *The American Musical: History and Development.* Mosaic Press, 2003.

For a comprehensive annotated bibliography as well as extensive further information about musicals, see www.musicals101.com.

Scripts

Scripts for a number of musicals are published in the following three American books which, although now out of print, may be available from libraries or second-hand book dealers:

Richards, S. (ed.) *Great Musicals of the American Theatre, Volume 1.* Chilton Book Co, 1973. Includes: *Of Thee I Sing; Porgy and Bess; One Touch of Venus; Brigadoon; Kiss Me, Kate; West Side Story; Gypsy; Fiddler on the Roof; 1176; Company.*

Richards, S. (ed.) *Great Musicals of the American Theatre, Volume 2.* Chilton Book Co, 1976. Includes: *A Little Night Music; Applause; Cabaret; Camelot; Fiorello; Lady in the Dark; Leave It To Me; Lost in the Stars; Man of La Mancha; Wonderful Town.*

Richards, S. (ed.) *Great Rock Musicals.* Stein and Day, 1979. Includes: *The Wiz; Two Gentlemen Of Verona; Grease; Jesus Christ Superstar; Your Own Thing; Hair; Tommy; Promenade.*